Praise for Benjamin Blech

". . . a biblical master."

David Sacks

Emmy Award-winning writer, producer

"Rabbi Benjamin Blech [is] a respected member of the Yeshiva University faculty and an articulate observer of human nature . . ."

Norman Lamm, Ph.D.

chancellor, Yeshiva University

". . . an inspiring spiritual leader . . . and a master teacher . . ."

Rabbi Emanuel Rackman

chancellor, Bar-Ilan University, Israel

"Rabbi Blech has . . . a unique ability to communicate the wisdom from our greatest repositories of knowledge and transform them into practical application for our everyday life!"

Morris Smith

former portfolio manager, Fidelity Magellan Fund

IF GOD IS GOOD
WHY IS THE WORLD SO BAD?

BENJAMIN BLECH

Deerfield Beach, Florida

www.simchapress.com

Library of Congress Cataloging-in-Publication Data

Blech, Benjamin.

If God is good why is the world so bad? / Benjamin Blech.

p. cm.

Includes bibliographical references.

Contents: pt. 1. Why bad things happen to good people. The dilemma of Job—Blame and guilt—The principle of greater priority—God's answer—pt. 2. Why we die. The price of paradise—The puzzle of death—Life after death—When a child dies—The gifts of aging, pain and illness—pt. 3. Why we suffer. Making sense of suffering—The test of Abraham—The balancing factor—Not of this world—The punishment of Moses—Faith after the Holocaust—A meeting with a mystic.

ISBN 0-7573-0123-1 (pbk.)

1. Suffering—Religious aspects—Judaism. 2. Death—Religious aspects—Judaism. I. Title.

BM645.S9B55 2003
296.3'118—dc21

2003052805

©2003 Benjamin Blech
ISBN 0-7573-0123-1

Simcha Press, its Logos and Marks are trademarks of Health Communications, Inc.

Publisher: Simcha Press
An Imprint of Health Communications, Inc.
3201 S.W. 15th Street
Deerfield Beach, FL 33442-8190

Cover design by Uri Berkowitz
Inside book design by Lawna Patterson Oldfield

This book is dedicated to all those
Who have inspired me and taught me by their example
That suffering can lead us closer
To God, to goodness, to compassion
And to greater understanding of ourselves and our lives

Special thanks to
Uriela Obst Sagiv
Who helped make this book possible

CONTENTS

PART III: WHY WE SUFFER

INTRODUCTION

The young woman with the troubled face stood in the back of the line of those waiting to speak to me. It seemed as if she wanted to be the last one. Sure enough, by the time it was her turn, the room was just about empty.

"Rabbi," she began with a sigh, "I have to speak to you." Her whole demeanor communicated pain, and I invited her to have a seat. Her story poured out.

After many attempts to get pregnant and several miscarriages, she had finally given birth to a baby girl. Her eyes filled with tears as she described her joy and subsequent pain on learning that the child had a number of congenital defects. She went on to tell me about the harrowing attempts to save the child's life, which ultimately failed. Her baby died.

"At the time, somebody gave me this book." She pulled out a paperback copy of *When Bad Things Happen to Good People,* the bestseller by Harold S. Kushner. "And it brought me a lot of comfort. It reassured me that what had happened was not my fault—that God didn't punish me or my baby."

She paused. "But now it gives me nightmares."

As she took a deep breath, I anticipated what was coming. I had heard it before.

"I now have two healthy children. We are so happy. But any minute now I expect something terrible to happen. If God doesn't run the world like this book says . . . ," her voice cracked and she tried hard to compose herself. "Rabbi, I don't know what to believe. Please help me make sense of it all."

How often had I been asked that very same question! In my nearly four decades as a rabbi, certainly no other problem has been addressed to me as often as this: Why do we suffer? Why do we die? Why my son? Why my mother? Why me?

Since the appearance of the now world-famous book *When Bad Things Happen to Good People,* countless people have asked me to explain: Does God run the world or doesn't He? Do bad things happen randomly, as Kushner maintains, or is there a plan and a design to the events of our lives?

Kushner, a Conservative rabbi, had written the book in the aftermath of the tragic death of his young son. In it, he tried to make sense of the little boy's terrible illness and of his own suffering. In his self-examination, he concluded that he had been a good person, and neither he nor his son had deserved such pain. That left him with a terrible dilemma—if God had willed this to happen, could God be good? He decided that God had to be good. So then, he reasoned, such a terrible thing could have happened to a good person only if the good God had been powerless to prevent it. *Bad things happen to good people because God is not in control of the world.*

In his conclusion, Kushner parted with some three thousand years of Jewish teaching. Additionally, Kushner made clear that he intentionally titled his book *When Bad Things Happen to Good People,* not *Why Bad Things Happen to Good People.* He has often stated—in his book and in his public lectures—that he is only interested in the aftermath: When it happens, what do you do? How do you recover from it? The why is both irrelevant and unanswerable.

Many people have no doubt found solace in Kushner's book. But over the years since it was published—and it is still in print and widely read—I have met countless individuals for whom this approach is far from satisfactory. Initially, his idea—that God does not run the world and bad things are not part of His plan—may seem appealing. After all, that allows us to believe we are not at fault for what happens to us. We bear no burden of guilt. We certainly can't blame ourselves for our suffering, if even God is incapable of making our lives any better.

But in the end, the feeling that the world is spinning out of control leaves one more frightened than ever. Nothing matters. There is no design. The lucky win. The unlucky perish. It is a gloomy, anarchistic view that most people intuitively recognize they cannot accept. Their souls tell them that it is simply not true.

No matter how cruel life may seem, people still somehow know that God *does* have unlimited power—or else He wouldn't be God. He *is* in control of the world. "So why?" people rightfully wonder. Why does the world seem so terrible? If God is good, why is life so bad?

Thankfully, ancient Jewish teachings provide answers. After all, it stands to reason that the most persecuted people in the world should be the greatest experts in dealing with the problem of suffering. Jews have been afflicted, brutalized, tortured and reviled throughout the ages. They have had cause to ask this question more than any other people. And it was God Himself who heard their cry and gave them the response through the teachings of the Torah as well as the writings of the prophets and teachers.

No, the answers are not simple. Nothing so perplexing can be resolved with a superficial explanation. Indeed, there are many answers, not one, and in different situations several may apply. The variables are endless, the combination of possibilities almost limitless.

Yet, I have confidence that what you are going to read will have meaning to any receptive heart. This book grew out of a lecture series that was exceptionally well received. One man in my audience summarized his feelings by saying, "What you did for me was not only make me understand my difficulties with much greater clarity, but you've also given me a powerful medicine for my soul."

In all honesty, speaking about this topic wasn't easy. I can safely say that this was the most difficult of all the subjects I have ever tackled in my lectures. Then, as I sat down to write about it, I had to do a lot of soul searching before I attempted the task. I realize that I've thankfully been spared major tragedies in my life. Although I had to cope with the deaths of my father and mother, both passed away at relatively advanced ages. The rest of my family, my wife and my children, are happy and healthy. Some people might say, "You haven't experienced real suffering. You don't really know."

There is some truth to that. But I did not intend this to be a self-help book written by a survivor for those suffering from the loss of a loved one or coping with critical illness. Rather, I wrote this book as a compilation of the Jewish wisdom on this subject. Absorbing the insights of the giants of our past—among them countless victims of suffering beyond compare who were nevertheless able to surmount their ordeals while maintaining their faith—I feel an overwhelming need to transmit what they have to teach us. Their understanding can transform our lives. Their observations can make our pain bearable. Because the hardest thing of all to accept as we are laid low by tragedy is that life, when all is said and done, has no meaning. And what the sages of old accomplished with their brilliance was to restore our ability to believe in a world of reason even when it appears painfully unreasonable.

What I am going to share with you are the fruits of thousands of years of debate, examination and spiritual struggle.

That said, let me clarify the sources I have used.

Primarily, the material I examine here comes from the Talmud. The Talmud is a large work of sixty volumes that expound Jewish commentary on the primary text, the Torah (the Five Books of Moses), believed to be the word of God. Additionally, the Talmud presents the lessons of the Midrash, a format of teaching deep lessons through stories, illustrations and parables.

It is very easy to tell a story; it is an entertaining, engaging way to teach. Students of the day were able to grasp difficult truths through the moral of the stories they heard. Later on, as the art of storytelling died out, Jewish philosophers—such as the famous Maimonides—would speak in more abstract terms. Which way of teaching is more correct? Whichever gets the point across better to the student, and all students are different. In this book we will make use of both, because each one has its place.

Finally, I'd like to note that while the subject of death and suffering may seem depressing, over the centuries Jews have—as odd as it might seem—found it uplifting and inspirational. Judaism is a religion that has as its chief mourning prayer a song—not of lament or sorrow, but of *praise* to God. Jewish mourners say a prayer known as *kaddish* after the death of a loved one. It begins: "May His great Name grow exalted and sanctified in the world that He created as He willed."

Having heard this prayer at a funeral, a non-Jewish participant once remarked to me in awe, "If Jews can praise God even in the presence of death, they must know something that the rest of the world doesn't."

It's true. Ancient Judaism teaches us how to acknowledge God's great name and His love for us at even the most terrible times. It affirms that there are rich and inspiring answers to the ultimate question: If God is good, why is life so bad?

Join with me as we start the most important spiritual journey of all—the quest for serenity in the face of adversity. And know that in the accumulated wisdom of the ages lies a time-tested solution for turning despair into hope and sorrow into faith for a better future.

PART I

WHY BAD THINGS HAPPEN TO GOOD PEOPLE

CHAPTER 1

THE DILEMMA
OF JOB

*"There was a man in the land of Uz
and his name was Job. . . ."*[1]

T hus begins one of the most famous of Biblical stories, the tale of a good and pious man, who, even when beset by calamity and tragedy, never falters in his allegiance to God.

As the narrative opens, Satan doubts Job's faith, telling God that Job's devotion is only due to his blessings. Job is healthy, wealthy and happy, but if his fortunes were to be reversed, Satan slyly suggests, his faith would not stand up to the trial. In response, God permits Satan to test Job, and he does so most cruelly. Job becomes penniless. His children die. He is afflicted with a terribly painful disease. And yet he refuses to curse God. Instead, he declares, "The Lord has given, and the Lord has taken away. Blessed be the name of the Lord."[2]

Friends admonish Job to repent for his sins, insisting that his tragedies must be divine punishment for wrongs he committed. Why else, they declare, could he be suffering this way? "Think now, what innocent man ever perished?" they ask him. "Where have the upright been destroyed?"[3] But Job knows he has done no wrong and refuses to repent. He pleads with God to explain why this evil has befallen him.

In the end, God rewards Job for his steadfastness by restoring his wealth in double measure, his family and his health. Job's friends are chastised for adding to Job's grief, and the story ends happily with Job living in contentment to the age of 140.

But Job never gets an answer. God's sole explanation for the suffering Job had to endure is a string of questions: "Where were you when I laid the Earth's foundations? . . . Can you send up an order to the clouds for an abundance of water to cover you? . . . Can you hunt prey for the lion and satisfy the appetite of the king of beasts? . . . Is it by your wisdom that the hawk grows pinions, spreads his wings to the south?"[4] In other words, God seems to be saying to Job, "I run this vast and complicated world, and you cannot possibly grasp the multitude of reasons why I do what I do."

And yet we continue to try. And it is Job's name that inevitably comes up when we struggle to understand why God allows evil in the world, when we ask the age-old question: Why do bad things happen to good people?

Surprisingly enough, the story may very well be fiction.

Job never existed, according to many of the sages of the Talmud.[5] So why is he in the Bible?

Although Job is perhaps the only imaginary hero of Biblical personalities, he is at the same time the most universal of all of them. He is the father who has inexplicably lost his job and has no means of supporting his family. He is the mother who has just been told her child has terminal cancer. He is the Holocaust survivor who still wakes up screaming in the middle of the night. He is me, and he is you.

That's why the book of Job is not really the story of a tragic figure of old. The book of Job is about twenty-first-century men and women who try to make sense out of the unfair circumstances of their lives even as they struggle to hold onto their beliefs. Most of all, the book of Job is about a dilemma which, sooner or later, every one of us must resolve in our lives. This dilemma is the apparent contradiction between three basic assumptions:

- God is just. He judges all of us with impartial fairness. He rewards the good, and He punishes the wicked.
- God is all-powerful. He can do anything. Nothing happens in the world without His willing it. Indeed, everything that happens is part of His plan.
- Job is a good man.

Now as long as everything is going well with Job—he is healthy and wealthy—we can believe all three of these statements at the same time with no difficulty. But when Job's suffering begins, when he loses his possessions, his family and his health, we have a problem. We can no longer make sense of all three propositions simultaneously. We can now affirm any two only by denying the third.

If God is both just and all-powerful, then it must be that the third statement is wrong—Job is not a good man; he is a sinner, and he deserves what is happening to him. But if Job is good and God causes his suffering nonetheless, then God cannot be just. Or if Job is good and God is not responsible for his suffering, then God cannot be all-powerful.

For all three to be true appears to be impossible. So which one is wrong? Which one of these three assumptions are we going to sacrifice on the altar of reality? That is the question.

IS GOD JUST?

For many, the most logical conclusion is that God is not just. God is capricious, perhaps even evil. Indeed, this was the prevailing worldview in ancient times when people worshiped gods like the Mayan ChacMool or the Mesopotamian Nergal—the precursor of our Satan. To these gods they sacrificed virgins, slaves and even their children—whatever it took to win the gods' appeasement.

For some, questioning God's justice takes a slightly different form: Although God is good, He must have an opponent who isn't, and who often prevails. This view inevitably leads to dualism, the belief that there are two gods—one a god of goodness and the other a god of evil. This is one of the oldest approaches to understanding the Divine and finding a rational response to the theological difficulty of evil. Zoroastrianism, the predominant religion of much of the Middle East from the time of the Persian Empire until the advent of Islam, accepted this view. We still see vestiges of it in those forms of Christianity that ascribe supernatural, godlike powers to Satan, the enemy of God. (In contrast, Judaism sees Satan as a servant of God whose function is to set up choices between good and evil so that we can exercise our free will.)

THE REAL MEANING OF MONOTHEISM

Abraham, the first monotheist, taught us that there is only one God. At the conclusion of his story in Genesis, the Bible tells us, "Abraham was now old, advanced in years, and the Lord had blessed Abraham in all things."[6]

And yet had God really blessed him in all things? Didn't God put him through ten difficult tests, the most staggering of which was the demand that he sacrifice his own son? Didn't Abraham have to wander the whole of the Fertile Crescent, endure famine and defend family members from attackers? Didn't he just bury his beloved wife Sarah, in the very sentences preceding this declaration that he was blessed "in all things"?

But Abraham was blessed in all things because he understood that a good God would only do things for his benefit. He saw every test, every difficulty, as an opportunity for self-improvement—a vehicle for the building of character, for the strengthening of faith, for moving closer to God. And therefore he considered everything that happened to him a blessing.

From the time of Abraham onward, the descendants and followers of the great patriarch proclaimed the oneness of God. The fundamental credo of Judaism states: *Shema Israel, Adonay Elohainu, Adonay Ehad.* "Hear O Israel, the Lord [is] Our God, the Lord is One." An observant Jew is required to repeat this credo twice a day, every day of his life. And these are the very last words that he is urged, if at all possible, to utter on his deathbed.

The question is obvious: Isn't this an odd way to express the oneness of God? If God is one, why does He have two names? Why is he called "Lord" and "God"—*Adonay* and *Elohainu* (the possessive form of *Elohim*)?

In this most basic expression of monotheism, the very struggle of man to understand the apparent contradiction of good and evil is addressed and answered. God is one, but He has two different attributes. Just as I am one person, while known at different times as Rabbi, Ben, Daddy, depending on the role I am filling, so too God is known alternatively as *Adonay* (translated Lord) and *Elohim* (translated God), depending on His function and the nature of His relationship at that particular moment. There are times that He appears to us as a loving father, exuding goodness and mercy; His name then is *Adonay,* to convey His quality of kindness. In English, we often say, "Thank the good Lord," because "Lord" is the proper translation for this name that stresses God's mercy.

But there are other times when He appears to us as a tough judge, meting out justice according to His law and punishing us for our infractions. Then His name is *Elohim,* "God," stern disciplinarian and unforgiving ruler of the universe. That's why, quite correctly, when we cry out in pain we say, "Oh my God" rather than "Oh my Lord."

But even though we describe Him by His two attributes, we know that in reality they are both aspects of one and the same loving Creator. The one who appears as strict disciplinarian is acting solely with the motivation of a kind and caring parent. In other words [to paraphrase]: "Hear O Israel, *(Adonay)* the Lord, and *(Elohainu)* our God, are actually *Adonay Ehad*, one Lord."

So the most basic tenet of Judaism states that of our three assumptions, we cannot reject the first. God is just and fair and good. His very essence is "Lord," even when He appears to be "God"; apparent harshness is merely camouflage for divine concern and love.

IS GOD ALL-POWERFUL?

Let's move to the second assumption, then. Maybe that's the one that's wrong. Maybe God isn't all-powerful. In *When Bad Things Happen to Good People,* Harold Kushner takes this stance. He argues that he would rather "diminish" God by saying that He is powerless to prevent bad things from happening than think badly of God for causing suffering. This is the lesser-of-two-evils stand. Floods, fires and tornadoes are not "acts of God," as insurance companies are fond of calling them, but random events. God is crying with us because He is helpless to ease our pain. There is nothing that He can do! The world as He has created it is on its own. Nature is haphazard and blind. Bacteria and viruses make no moral choices about whom they will infect. Chromosomes mutate by chance, and a deformed child is born. Engines fail and planes crash without rhyme or reason. God was "First Cause," but after creation, He no longer chooses—or even has the ability—to get involved.

Traditional Judaism forcefully rejects this view. At times God may willfully limit His power to act in order to grant us free will, but He is never weak or impotent. The power of God and the personal, *direct involvement* of God in the world are expressed in the very first of the Ten Commandments: "I am the Lord, your God, who has taken you out of the land of Egypt, the house of bondage." God does not identify Himself as the Creator of heaven and Earth who set the world in motion and then left it to randomly evolve. God announces Himself as the planner of the Ten Plagues that broke the Egyptian resolve to enslave the Israelites. To free His people, He cowed the mightiest empire on Earth.

But God is clearly communicating even more than that in the opening words of the Decalogue. For one thing, in the nineteen chapters preceding the Ten Commandments, the Bible relates in great detail the ordeal of the Israelites in Egypt and their miraculous rescue. This additional reminder that God was their redeemer is hardly necessary. Also, there seems to be a redundancy—"the land of Egypt" followed by "the house of bondage," as if we needed more clarification. The Ten Commandments are considered the most concise summary of Judaism, so why "land" *and* "house"?

The first of the Ten Commandments, by way of this dual expression, is in fact teaching us an all-important idea about the *way* in which God is involved in the world. There are those who might be willing to admit that God plays a role in history, but find it impossible to believe that His concern extends beyond nations to include every single person. God, they think, is willing to busy Himself with "big things" like the fate of an entire people, but surely not with what happens to every individual family. Theologically, they have no problem accepting God as the One who would take all of the Jews out of the "land of Egypt"; what they have trouble believing is that God is so involved in details that He's also concerned with every "house of bondage." Land, yes, but house, no. The Exodus demonstrated that God saved not only the Jewish people, but also every Jewish person. That's why, before leaving Egypt together as a nation, the Jews were commanded to mark the doorposts of their homes. They were told to slaughter a lamb, an Egyptian god, to prove their rejection of idolatry. They had to take the blood of that lamb and smear it on their doorposts to publicly acknowledge their commitment as well as their trust in God. If they did that, God promised He would *take note of every household and have the angel of death* "pass over" the homes of those who chose to identify with Him.

Yes, God knew every address, every resident. In that immense display of His power to change history, He also demonstrated the most intimate kind of caring. He intervened not just to save a people, but to rescue six hundred thousand individuals—each and every one of them a precious micro-cosm of the entire world and a beloved child of his or her Creator.

To attest to this incredible fact, Jews to this day celebrate the festival of Passover. At a feast called a *Seder* (meaning "order"), the story of the Israelites' liberation is read and re-enacted. What parents try to teach their children is that for every event of life, whether large or small, there is a reason, because the "principle of divine order" rules everything that happens.

So we also can't reject the second of the three assumptions: God *is* all-powerful. He is the author of history—and His divine maxim is *not* "mind your own business."

IS JOB GOOD?

As you can see, there's only one assumption left to explain the riddle of Job's affliction: Job must be a bad person after all. You'll recall that's what Job's friends concluded as well. It is the same kind of logic that remarkably enough found an echo after the Holocaust by those who subscribe to what I call "theological Holocaust revisionism." Frankly, it is an approach that I see as even more dangerous and despicable than the view that claims the Holocaust didn't happen. The latter is easily refutable; the former condemns those who have no opportunity to respond on their own behalf.

To claim that the victims deserved their fate appalls me. Not only were those 6 million people tortured and murdered, not only did they have everything precious to them destroyed and desecrated, but now after death, their memories are defiled by those who say, "They must have deserved it." Could 6 million men, women and children possibly have deserved such a fate? Were they all so evil? Even the children?

AN ALTERNATIVE EXPLANATION

Could it be that all three assumptions are correct, and there is another way to solve the dilemma that Job presents?

The answer is yes.

CHAPTER 2

BLAME AND GUILT

To find the solution to the dilemma of Job, we must turn to the ancient wisdom of the Talmud.

Posing the question—if a person suffers, must that mean he or she deserves it?—we immediately get two seemingly contradictory answers.

In the Tractate Baba Metzia,[7] while expounding on the harm that can be inflicted with words, the Talmud explains what the Bible means when it condemns the sin of "oppressing a stranger." It offers this example: "If someone is visited by suffering, afflicted with disease or has buried his children, one must not speak to him as his companions spoke to Job: '. . . Think now, what innocent man ever perished?'"

Clearly, the Talmud condemns the friends of Job who told him he must have committed some crime to deserve his suffering. The rabbis consider their behavior in the category of those who oppress others with words.

But in the Tractate Berakhot,[8] the Talmud teaches: "If a man sees that painful suffering visit him, let him examine his conduct, for it is said: 'For I give you good instruction; do not forsake my teaching.'" In other words, God gives us "teachings" in life that we must interpret for their message. Our suffering may well be a consequence of our sinful actions.

So what are we to make of these two seemingly contradictory Talmudic passages? Is suffering the deserved consequence of sin, or are the two totally unrelated?

In the first source, we are admonished not to jump to the same conclusion as the friends of Job that someone who is suffering is being punished for something he did wrong. Yet in the second passage we are told that if an individual is visited by tragedy, he must try to figure out what it is that he did wrong. How can we reconcile these diametrically opposite statements?

In truth, there is no real contradiction here. In both instances the suffering *may* or *may not* be the consequence of one's actions. But there is a major difference between using tragedy to find fault with others and having tragedy enlighten us with regard to our own failings.

Clearly, the Talmud is saying that no individual can judge anyone else and deduce from the mere presence of suffering that this is God's punishment for sin. It may or may not be true. Someone can suffer and still be good. Even the pious know pain, and even the saintly endure sickness. There are a whole host of reasons that might explain this, as we will discover, all of which in no way reflect on the virtue of the person who's suffering. You don't dare condemn and malign a decent human being.

But if *you* are that individual who is suffering, you *do* have an obligation to ask yourself: What *might* I have done to deserve this? What could I have done to bring this on? Is it possible that my suffering *is* a punishment from God? Or is it possible that my suffering is perhaps a message, a wake-up call to which I must respond?

Simply put, the Talmud teaches us to react to suffering in two different ways, depending on whether we are looking at others or ourselves. The proper response to the suffering of others is *compassion;* we are forbidden to condemn. The correct reaction to our own suffering is *introspection;* perhaps God is simply using a painful method to convey to us an important truth.

And how can we know whether our own suffering is divine punishment or heavenly warning? When God intervenes, when He is sending you a message, you will know it. How? There is one sure way to tell—God is very specific and leaves no doubt about His meaning if you merely give it a little thought.

LOUD AND CLEAR

I will give you some very simple examples of unmistakable messages from God involving people I know.

A young woman wanted to study in Israel, but the cost of the trip—$1,450—was beyond her parents' means. The father prayed for God's help, because he thought this was an important thing for his daughter to do. Then he got the idea to clean out some junk behind a store he owned and to hold a rummage sale. Maybe, he hoped, the proceeds would raise some of the funds. At the end of the sale, he totaled up what he took in—exactly $1,450. It was too remarkable to be a coincidence. Obviously, God approved this decision and saw to it that it could be realized.

In the family of a friend of mine, the grandfather had a tradition of financing all the bar mitzvahs of his grandsons. When my friend's son was preparing to celebrate his entry into manhood, the grandfather, of course, wanted to cover the cost, as was his custom. My friend argued with him, but the grandfather would not be dissuaded. Unfortunately, just months before the bar mitzvah took place, the grandfather died. My friend could well afford to pay for his son's bar mitzvah, but around that time he bought a lottery ticket and won. The amazing thing was that when the caterer's bill came, for a total of exactly $2,365, so did his lottery winnings, minus the taxes, for $2,365. "My grandfather's prayers have been answered after all," he said. "He paid for the bar mitzvah."

Again, the correlation was too exact to be simple chance. As you can see, there are times when God wants us to clearly recognize that He is intervening in our lives. To do so, He utilizes what I would call the "preciseness of statistical impossibility." What is too far-fetched to be coincidence must be nothing other than divine intervention. As the profound observation goes, "Coincidence is simply God's way of choosing to remain anonymous."

Although I was aware of this concept, I wasn't prepared for the moment when it so clearly happened to me.

On a trip to Eastern Europe to visit the places where my ancestors lived, as well as the concentration camps where much of my family perished, I spent one Sabbath morning in a synagogue in Warsaw. The custom is for a few people in the congregation to be given the great honor of coming up to the Torah and reciting the appropriate blessings. I didn't identify myself as a rabbi, but for some reason, of all the tourists as well as local residents, they selected me as one of the seven designated honorees.

It is also the custom for the people given this honor to publicly make a pledge of a donation for the synagogue. As I concluded my blessings and was emotionally overcome by the realization of where I was and how many great Jewish leaders must have preceded me standing at this very spot, I felt the need to make a very generous contribution. I hesitated, however, because I didn't want to appear like a rich American tourist shaming all the other honorees whose contributions were limited by their lesser means. As a compromise in my own mind between these conflicting desires, I decided that a pledge of thirty-six American dollars would be just about right—enough to be meaningful as a gift and not exorbitant as an expression of ego. No sooner was the pledge announced than there was an audible gasp from the congregants. It seems that thirty-six

American dollars was quite a fortune in the currency of Polish *zlotys*. The president quickly came over to me, asked where I was staying, and if it would be all right for a committee to come to my hotel immediately after the Sabbath to collect this generous donation. Of course I agreed, and within five minutes after the Sabbath ended with the appearance of three stars in the heavens, the committee appeared in the lobby and asked me to make good on my pledge. I happily gave them the money and felt very pleased that I had the merit of being able to perform a good deed, a *mitzvah*.

My wife and I then wondered what there was to do to while away a few hours on a Saturday night in Warsaw. The concierge told us there was a casino on the premises and that was about the only activity available to us.

New to gambling, I stopped at the very first slot machine and, on a lark, deposited one coin. What followed was indescribable. Lights flashed, gongs went off, people around the room stopped what they were doing to see what had happened. I stood amazed as money kept pouring out of the machine. It seems I hit the jackpot, and I quickly kept filling bucket after bucket with my winnings. I immediately decided that I must have used up my share of good luck for that night, and I went to cash in my winnings.

The cashier put all the coins through her counting machine and finally came up with a total. The sum she told me was staggering, and for a moment I thought I was almost a millionaire. What I had forgotten was that the amount she told me was in Polish currency, *zlotys*. Anxiously, I asked her, "What does that come to in American dollars?"

After some quick calculating, she replied, "Oh, about thirty-six American dollars."

For years I had preached that whatever we give eventually comes back to us. But this time God made it so abundantly clear that my contribution was rewarded by its exact equivalent. I had heard similar stories from others and always found them hard to believe. Now I knew firsthand that God is to be found not only in synagogues and houses of worship, but even in Las Vegas, Atlantic City and a casino in Warsaw!

THE MEASURE-FOR-MEASURE PRINCIPLE

Let us now suppose that the event is not a happy one, as in the previous examples. There are times when misfortune, rather than good fortune, strikes and God's hand is clearly behind it. When is a painful message from God a direct punishment for wrongs committed?

The principle is the same: The correlation will be precise. You will be able to easily match the "punishment" with the "crime"; they will be clearly linked by content and context.

The Torah gives us a number of such examples. Perhaps the most famous happens in the book of Exodus. As you may recall, the Egyptians, in their persecution of the Israelites, drowned thousands of Jewish babies. Then, when the Israelites fled and the Red Sea parted to grant them safe passage, it was the pursuing Egyptians who were drowned. No one could miss the connection. It was a specific message from God that this was a punishment, and the crime that caused it was undoubtedly identified by the manner of their destruction.

Another illustration from the Torah comes from a story of Jacob, the last of the patriarchs. In order to obtain the parental blessing of the firstborn from his father Isaac—a blessing that he felt he deserved and had previously purchased from his brother Esau—Jacob deceived his blind father. Some time later, after working for his uncle Laban for seven years in order to win the hand of his beloved cousin Rachel, he found himself the victim of an act of deception. Laban switched the bride at the last moment and substituted his elder daughter, Leah. The one who fooled others was now fooled. Fate—or better put, "the finger of God"—assured recompense for a wrong, even when committed by an otherwise blameless person.

In the Talmud, this principle is known as "measure for measure"—meaning that according to God's justice the punishment always fits the crime.

It's a concept that makes itself known quite often in our own lives if we're only wise enough to acknowledge it and to listen to its message. Just a short while ago, a man came to me with a sheepish look on his face. A couple of weeks before, I had approached this wealthy businessman to ask him for a contribution of $460 to help out in a situation that was a literal life-and-death emergency. He had turned me down. Now he confided to me, "Rabbi, when I said no to you, I knew that I was wrong. A day later inspectors came to my place of business—something that's never happened before—and fined me a total of $460 for infractions that turned out to be mistakenly attributed to me. I guess God just wanted to prove to me that I didn't deserve that money anymore. I just wish I would have given it to you."

So, this is a principle we can rely on whenever it speaks to us with a clear sign that it's measure for measure. When we suffer, it may or may not be the consequence of a wrong committed. But no one else has a right to make that judgment. However, the sufferer himself should take inventory. He should see if there is any correlation. Is God sending him a specific, unmistakable message? If the punishment fits the crime, the pain is a call for repentance!

WARNING: BEWARE

I must add a few words of caution here. Don't overreact in your self-examination. Jewish guilt is the punch line of many a joke, but it's not a funny matter when irrational guilt causes irreparable harm. Guilt out of proportion to the "crime" is not part of the teachings of Judaism. Yet some people, because they have been poorly taught, because they have somehow acquired a twisted idea of God, because they believe that God exacts His "pound of flesh" no matter what, erroneously take on a level of guilt that is illogical and seriously harmful. By confusing their own petty failings with capital crimes, they condemn themselves to self-inflicted torture far beyond anything that would be decreed by a compassionate God.

A woman I know was sexually promiscuous as a college student, but felt no guilt about it at the time. Among her peers, in the hippie culture of "free love," casual sex was normal behavior. As she matured, she left that lifestyle behind and became religiously committed. When, at a synagogue social, she met the man of her dreams, she felt no need to confess to him her youthful indiscretions. She was happily married for two years when her husband was killed in a car accident. Her grief knew no bounds. Searching for a reason why this tragedy was visited upon her, she convinced herself that God "killed" her husband to punish her for her illicit past. She eventually suffered a nervous breakdown.

Obviously, her assumption of guilt was completely irrational. How could this, by any stretch of the imagination, be considered "measure for measure"? Unfortunately, extreme guilt reactions such as this are not uncommon. Therefore, I want to be most emphatic: People like this woman couldn't be more wrong. If her loss was indeed punishment, it most certainly didn't fit the crime. Yet people who think as she did destroy themselves, destroy their families, destroy their mates and destroy their children because of a level of guilt they assume without any foundation. It is bad enough to suffer the initial tragedy. What is often far worse is to create yet another tragedy for yourself by thinking that "I must have deserved it" when it clearly could not be true. Self-blame at this level makes a person feel totally unworthy—unworthy of life, unworthy of giving to others, unworthy of doing anything, unworthy of being. Such a person has decided that of our three assumptions, it is the third that is wrong. "I am not a good person. A just and all-powerful God has punished me for my sins." Yet, we have demonstrated that this was not true in the case of Job, and it is most certainly not always true when people suffer.

To attest otherwise is to be guilty of *accusing oneself falsely,* and this act of bearing false witness, whether done against oneself or one's neighbor, is expressly forbidden by the ninth of the Ten Commandments. What's more, it also involves bearing false witness against God, because a just God exacts his punishment—when He does so—with fairness, according to the principle of measure for measure.

IN SUMMARY

Let us see how far we are in answering the question: Why do good people suffer?

We have to believe that God is good and just and that God is all-powerful. To believe otherwise is to no longer have a God to whom we can pray. Why pray to a God who is impotent to respond? Few of us who believe in God would accept that view.

When we see other people suffer, we must withhold judgment. We must give them the benefit of the doubt, because we do not know why this is happening to them. But if we are the ones suffering, we are obligated to engage in sincere introspection. Could this hurt be a message from God?

God does occasionally send us a painful message for our own good, in a way that can help us to better live our lives. If you touch fire, what happens? You feel a painful burning sensation, and you pull your hand away before some serious damage is done. Suffering may be that kind of message. But you should trust that if this is so, there will be a clue in the message. You will be able to see some link between what happened to you and something that you did wrong that bothers you deep in your gut. For example, if some years ago you cheated a client or business partner and then tomorrow someone cheats you, you have a clear correlation. That's a clue.

But if there is no such linkage, or if the suffering seems far out of proportion to anything you may have done in life, then do not—I repeat *do not*—heap guilt upon yourself. There are many other reasons why you may be suffering, as we shall see in the succeeding chapters.

CHAPTER 3

THE PRINCIPLE OF GREATER PRIORITY

I n the beginning, God created the heaven and the Earth. And the Earth was void and desolate, and darkness covered the surface of the abyss. And the spirit of God hovered above the face of the waters."[9]

These are the opening sentences of the Bible that go on to tell us the dramatic story of how we came to be. Remarkably, from the outset we are given a very important clue as to how God will relate to His creation and to our pain and suffering. The clue lies in the unusual Hebrew word *m'rachefet,* meaning "hovered," which appears in the entire Bible only twice—here and at the very end of the Pentateuch, in the book of Deuteronomy.[10] There, Moses, in describing to the Israelites the relationship of God to His people, compares God to an eagle that *hovers* over its young.

The famed Biblical commentator Rashi clarifies the comparison by explaining, "The eagle does not press itself on the young, but hovers, touching yet not touching." Were the eagle to rest on the young, it would smother them.

In our society we all have witnessed the tragedy of mother love turned into smother love. There are parents whose love crushes the child, smothering every aspect of the child's initiative and freedom, so that it becomes totally dependent on its parents for the rest of its life.

An old joke effectively illustrates this extreme in over-protectiveness: A woman pulls up in a limousine in front of a fancy department store, and the chauffeur steps up to carry out her ten-year-old son. A passerby remarks, "Oh, what a tragedy. The boy can't walk." The mother overhears and becomes angry, "What do you mean, 'can't walk'? He doesn't have to!"

To learn to walk a child must fall and hurt himself. After much trying and a few bumps and bruises, he will finally stand up on his feet and take a step. But the mother described in the joke couldn't bear watching her child's pain. So she has ensured that he will never stand on his own two feet.

Of course, all mothers and fathers have a hard time watching their children learning to walk. You see the kid stand up, take a step and . . . boom . . . he gets a nasty bruise. So what do you want to do? You want to grab the child; you want to say, "Don't do it again." But he can only learn to walk if you let him fall.

So this is the decision that God has made at the very beginning of creation. He will let us fall so we can learn to walk.

He will hover over us, He will protect us, but He will not smother us. He will be there directing, guiding, helping, but not controlling.

To love somebody means letting that person be himself or herself. The name for that aspect of God's love—for that gift which He gave humankind so that we could be ourselves—is free will.

If humankind did not have free will, we would still be in the Garden of Eden, because we could not have chosen to disobey God's one commandment not to eat of the Tree of Knowledge of Good and Evil. But without that freedom to choose, our lives would have been a puppet show, directed, staged and produced by God Himself. God did not want that. So instead God gave man free will, and as soon as He did, man took matters into his own hands.

The first thing that man did was to eat from the forbidden tree, the price for which was mortality. And mortality brought with it pain and suffering.

Did God want man to stay in the Garden of Eden and enjoy the bliss there? The answer is yes. God had told the first human beings very clearly what would happen if they ate of the Tree of Knowledge of Good and Evil. But they chose to exercise their free will and travel a path that carried with it some very grave consequences.

So from one of the very first stories in the Bible we learn that sometimes there are things that happen in the world that God does not want to see happen, but He allows them to happen nevertheless. If God were to interfere each and every time, He would be smothering us and denying us free will.

FREEDOM TO KILL

The very fact that God has given us a commandment, "Thou shalt not murder," shows that we have a choice whether to do it or not to do it. God tells us, "Don't do it, because the consequences of such an act will be very severe," but we can still do it if we want to.

Now if a person makes a choice to murder another human being, he may very well succeed. Yet it is quite possible, if not probable, that God did not want the victim to die. This has very important bearing on why bad things happen to good people, as we shall soon see.

We learn in the book of Exodus[11] the difference between premeditated murder and accidental killing. The punishment for the former is death; the punishment for the latter is exile to a "city of refuge" where the offender could live and study amongst spiritual people before returning home.

The man who commits murder is clearly exercising his free will. The man who kills accidentally is not. Indeed, the original Hebrew phrase that is translated as "accidentally" literally says, "God brought it to his hand." It is only the death by accident that is the will of God; death by intentional murder is not.

Mind you, the fellow who kills by accident may not be such a good man, which is why God chose him for this purpose.

That's what King David teaches us in the *Proverb of the Ancient One:* "Wickedness emanates from the wicked," which the rabbis in the Midrash[12] explain with this insightful story:

There were two men, one who committed murder and another who killed someone accidentally. There were no witnesses, so neither one had to suffer the consequences of his actions—at least for a time. As it happened, God caused the two men to meet at an inn. There the man who had killed accidentally climbed a ladder, and the murderer sat under it. The man at the top of the ladder slipped and fell, killing the murderer sitting beneath. Thus God punished the murderer with death, and the accidental killer was sent to the "city of refuge" as he should have been in the first place.

What we learn is that there is no escaping the consequences of our actions, even if for a time we manage to go against God's will by our freedom of choice.

Now we have a *partial* answer to our question (and I stress the word "partial," because this is a very complicated matter which we are unraveling bit by bit): If it isn't God's will, why do men die? Because if God were to prevent every person from doing something if it might cause an innocent to suffer, it would mean that God would have to protect good people at the expense of the principle of free will. Given the choice, God chooses to have no choice.

I call this the "principle of greater priority." God's priority is that man should have free will. But that should not suggest that ultimately God's wishes will be thwarted or that injustice will rule the world, because God has a way of working everything out in the end. It does suggest, however, that in order to exercise his free will, man will do things that are not pleasing in the eyes of God. Indeed, man will do things that can cause God pain.

The Talmud tells us that there are times when God "cries," God "hopes," God "waits anxiously," God "suffers." When the sages of the Talmud use such words, they are speaking metaphorically, of course, in order to convey the idea that often our actions are not in keeping with God's wishes. God does not play games with us; He gave us laws to live by, with consequences clearly spelled out. But when the choices of some people cause others pain, God who loves us all hurts with us. And yet, like the mother who wrings her hands as her child falls and gets bruised but lets it happen because that is the only way the child will learn to walk, God hovers over us, watching anxiously, but not interfering when our free will would be compromised.

GOD'S JUSTICE

In the opening chapter of this book, we refused to reject the assumption that God is just and the assumption that God is all-powerful. So now we must ask the question: If God chooses to limit His power so that man can exercise his free will, how is justice served?

I know of a case involving a rabbi and his wife who were in a very serious car wreck caused by a drunken driver. Not only were the rabbi and his wife badly hurt, but many others were indirectly affected as well. His wife suffered a broken arm, nose and a fracture of the spinal vertebrae, which required hospitalization for weeks. During her lengthy recovery, many people who depended on her love and caring, including her aged parents, also suffered.

The rabbi followed our initial rule to examine if this painful happenstance could be a message from God, but he could find no correlation. He concluded that if God had wanted to punish him for some wrongdoing, he surely would not have caused so many other people to suffer. God had not wanted the car wreck to happen, but God did not interfere with the choices of the drunken driver.

Yet the rabbi recognized God's presence at the scene. He wrote of it later: "God was in the hearts of those wonderful strangers who interrupted their journeys to come to the aid of two wounded travelers they did not know. God was in the ambitions of the paramedics who had dedicated themselves to help people even when their own lives were threatened. God was in the emergency room, ministering through the trained minds, the caring hands and the consoling words. God was in the hearts of the generous people who built the hospital. And God was in the prayers of the people who cared for them."

That is all well and good, you might say, but if the rabbi did not deserve this suffering and God is angry and sad that it happened, does He not have some obligation to see justice done? Or can God just ignore what happened?

The answer, of course, is that God *must* somehow get involved. God "owes" the rabbi. God has an obligation to rectify the undeserved harm that the victim in this situation had suffered.

The way I picture it, we all have a kind of bank account with God. There are times when withdrawals, have to be made. Sometimes, we don't want these withdrawals, but they are made and then God owes us.

You might say to God, "I would have preferred not to have been in this car wreck. I didn't need this broken leg just now to impede the good work I'm doing."

And God might answer, "You are right. You didn't need it. And you didn't deserve it. I didn't want this to happen to you. But since it did happen, I've got to be fair to you. So I will make it up to you as fast as I can. To start with, I will make you understand something about other people that perhaps you never understood until now. I will teach you new insights about life as a result of this car wreck, so that in the end you will say that what happened to you was a blessing."

To get the phone calls of empathy and concern, to suddenly see ordinary people do extraordinary things for you, to get an awareness of the goodness of people, all these are worth something. I am not saying they justify everything. But God is just—when He owes you, He will make good on it. There will be a repayment in full measure, and you can count on it!

EXCEPTIONS TO THE RULE

God has decided that we should have free will. But let us suppose that through an exercise of one's free will, all of us would cease to exist. One madman has reached the button that could unleash a nuclear holocaust and destroy the planet. Would God intervene?

I'm certain He would. He would have no other choice because He made an irrevocable commitment to our survival.

This is one of the all-important lessons of the Biblical book of Esther. God had promised Abraham and Moses[13] that the Jewish people would be an "eternal nation" never to be destroyed. And yet during the time of the Persian Empire, there appeared a very powerful minister, Haman, who hated the Jews and decided to destroy them. Indeed, it seemed that Haman had not only the free will, but also the means to succeed in his endeavor.

Were God to allow Haman to exercise his free will, He would have had to make it up to the Jewish people at some later point. But when the intended crime isn't just murder but genocide, there might not be any Jewish people left to make it up to. Such a thing simply cannot happen. It conflicts with God's own promise, which must take priority.

Therefore the miracle of Purim had to take place. And it is very interesting to see just how God caused it to happen. Queen Esther turned out to be very instrumental in saving the Jewish people. At first, she was not sure if she was prepared for the dangers of the mission, until her uncle Mordechai told her, "If you keep silent in this crisis, relief and deliverance will come to the Jews from another quarter."[14] So even Esther had a chance to exercise her free will as to whether or not she would participate in God's salvation. Had she decided not to, God would have found another person or another method. Esther did, of course, and not only was Haman's plan foiled, but he was the one who perished.

Similarly, Hitler was another free agent who wanted to destroy all the Jews. His plan almost succeeded. He killed 6 million, but he never succeeded in carrying out his "Final Solution." Stories of miraculous rescues during the war abound, and Yaffa Eliach has collected nearly one hundred of them in her book *Hassidic Tales of the Holocaust.* These were the beneficiaries of divine intervention made necessary for God to prevent the negation of His promise to the patriarchs.

One of the more amazing of these stories tells of a terrible morning at Janowska Road Camp, when the Jewish inmates, exhausted from hard labor, starvation and disease, were assembled around a huge pit, soon to be their common grave. Taking cruel sport, the Nazis told the people that if anyone could jump across the pit—an impossible feat—this person's life would be spared. One young man standing next to an old rabbi suggested that they defy the Nazis and refuse to jump. But the rabbi said, "No, we must jump." And so they closed their eyes and jumped.

When they opened their eyes again, they were on the other

side of the pit, safe and sound. The only way possible that they could have made it is to have flown. "Tell me, Rabbi, how did you do it?" the young man asked in amazement.

"I imagined I was holding onto the coattails of my father, my grandfather and my great-grandfather, of blessed memory," the rabbi replied. And then he asked the young man, "Tell me, my friend, how did *you* reach the other side of the pit?"

The young man smiled. "I was holding onto you."

God did not save everybody in the Holocaust. That is true. He did not make miracles all the time, nor for everyone. But whoever died has made a withdrawal from the bank, and God owes those people nothing less than their lives. How it is possible for them to be repaid we will see shortly.

IN SUMMARY

In the beginning of this book, we decided that the assumption that God is all-powerful is true. God runs the world. And in this chapter we have not wavered from that stance. If a brick falls off a ledge and kills a passerby below, if an earthquake collapses a building and people are killed, if any accident occurs, we have to assume that God willed that to happen.

But God also decided at the very beginning of creation that he will "hover" over human beings. He will let us be ourselves. Whenever a human being's freedom of will is involved, God, of necessity, keeps a hands-off policy.

That's why, under normal circumstances, God will not interfere. However, miracles are always possible. God is all-powerful, and when a greater priority overrides man's gift of free will, God doesn't hesitate to do what must be done. Miracles are God's answer to free will gone wild, threatening to destroy God's Master Plan for the world.

There are countless situations where people drive themselves to the brink of a nervous breakdown because they cannot find the answer to the question, "Why did God do this to me?" They convince themselves that God has written them off, and their lives are not worth living. These people are wrong. Sometimes the tragedy that was visited upon them had nothing to do with God. It was the fault of a human being who, exercising his free will, caused them harm. And if they are blameless—if having examined their past, they can say there was no correlation with a wrongdoing in their past— then they are entitled to the following comfort: God did not want this to happen, and He will make good on it.

Most of the time, the greater priority for God is preserving our free will. But there are times when an even greater priority is God's promise to the past and His commitment to the future. In those cases, the free will of man can and must be curtailed.

If human history on a grand scale is involved, if survival of the universe is involved, if the survival of the Jewish people is involved, if an upright person whom God needs for some part of His divine plan is involved, then God *will* intervene. God will split the Red Sea, make the sun stand still and even let people jump over mountains.

But in the normal scheme of things, free will can cause a great deal of harm to innocent people. You may suffer a loss that God Himself cries over. For that you must know that God assumes the obligation to make up to you the injustice of evil that He permitted. And if you ask how, know that for God nothing is impossible.

For those who believe that God is powerless, prayer is a delusion. Why pray when God can't change things anyway? But for those of us who believe in an all-powerful God, prayer offers a fountain of hope. Miracles are possible, and one can pray for a miracle. Even when man's free will is involved and He normally would not intervene, He can make a miracle when it's absolutely necessary. And you're permitted to pray that you are in an absolutely necessary situation. If you have already suffered a loss, you can remind God that He has a debt to repay. God can make it up to you. I don't know exactly how, but He will do something. He owes you one. Pray to Him to help you. Don't condemn Him. Pray to Him to help you in the situation as it is.

As you can see by now, there are many reasons why bad things happen to good people. Each situation is unique and complex. We are examining one aspect at a time—patiently exposing little pieces of the great mosaic—but we have yet to see the whole picture. . . .

CHAPTER 4

GOD'S ANSWER

We have just seen that much of what troubles us about God's ways should really be ascribed to the actions of man. But what about the times when the evil stems directly from God?

What if a doctor informs you that your child has incurable cancer? Nobody has hurt your child. This evil seems to be coming from the One who supposedly does only good. If an evil person had hurt your child, you may not be able to forgive him, but you would at least know where to place the blame—on human wickedness. But if God has hurt your child, that is simply too much to bear.

Yet little, innocent children suffer every day. And invariably we are led to ask: How can a good God be so utterly cruel?

What troubles us also troubled the greatest Jewish leader, Moses. He dared to ask this question to The One Who Knows the Answer. And that eternal wisdom is shared with us in the book of Exodus. It is here, the Talmud tells us, that the Bible first takes up the problem of why the righteous suffer.

At first glance the passage may appear cryptic:

> *Moses then said [to God], "Please grant me a vision of Your Glory." He [God] said, "I will cause all My goodness to pass before you and will proclaim the name of the Lord in your presence. I will be gracious to whom I will be gracious, and I will be compassionate to whom I will be compassionate." And He said, "You cannot see My Presence and live." And the Lord said, "Behold, there is a place alongside Me, and you shall set yourself on the rock. When My Glory passes by, I will put you in a cleft of the rock, and I will cover you with My Hand until I pass by. Then I will remove My Hand and you will see My Back, but My Face shall not be seen."*[15]

Most people who are reading this literally assume that Moses is asking to know what God looks like, and, in answer, God won't show His face, but lets Moses take a peek at His mighty shoulder blades.

That is, of course, absurd.

The Talmud[16] tells us that Moses was not asking to "see" God. Moses knew better. Moses knew that God has no body or any form for that matter and therefore cannot be seen with human eyes. Rather Moses was asking to "see" God's "glory," so that he could understand God's plan. In effect, Moses is saying to God, "God, I love, honor and respect You in every way. But there are things about You that I do not understand. When I see a child with infantile paralysis, when I see a baby with leukemia, when I see a little boy suffering great pain and I know he is going to die soon, I don't know what You are doing. And I would love to have a total understanding of Your ways so that I can give you the full honor You deserve."

It is very significant that this passage appears right after God's absolution of the Israelites for the terrible sin of the golden calf. God had led the Israelites out of the slavery of Egypt; He had performed astonishing miracles before their eyes; He had spoken to them at Mount Sinai; and then, when Moses went up the mountain, the Israelites repaid all this goodness by rejecting God and building an idol. Yet when they atoned for this great sin, He had not only forgiven them, but also responded by describing His essence as being one of complete mercy and compassion.

That is when Moses chose to make his request, as if to say, "If that is true, then will You explain how Your glory is reflected in the suffering of children and in the gloating of the wicked? Can you give me the gift of seeing how that makes sense?"

In short, Moses wanted to know why bad things happen to good people.

God's answer contains what Moses, as well as all of us reading these words thousands of years later, have the right to know.

So let us look very carefully, point by point, at what God is telling us.

THE WHOLE PICTURE

"I will cause all My goodness to pass before you and will proclaim the name of the Lord in your presence."

As we learned earlier, the names by which God identifies Himself are extremely important. Here, He uses the unique four-letter name known as the Tetragrammaton, which we are forbidden to pronounce; it is generally translated as Lord *(Adonay).* As noted earlier, this name signifies kindness and compassion, as contrasted with the name *Elohim,* which refers to God as the harsh but just judge. So it is the name of the merciful Lord that He wishes to proclaim to Moses.

We are told that "all" of God's goodness will be testimony to the merciful quality of the Almighty. And, by implication, that we will change our perception of pain and suffering once we have seen it "all." Seeing only half the story leads us to think God is cruel, but a fuller perspective will let us grasp why every strict judgment was really a necessary act of love.

Once we are able to understand the whole picture, we will see suffering as a manifestation of the compassionate side of God.

"I will be gracious to whom I will be gracious, and I will be compassionate to whom I will be compassionate."

Is God saying, "I will do whatever I want regardless of what is just"? No, He is not saying that. But He is saying, "I will be gracious to the one I will be gracious to, and *not* to the one *you think* I should be gracious to. I will be compassionate to whom I will be compassionate, and not to the one you think I should be compassionate to."

The Talmud teaches[17] that in the world-to-come everything will be turned upside down. Those who are on the bottom here will be on top there and vice versa. The point it makes is that very often our judgments about who is a saint and who is a sinner are far off the mark. The way the world offers honor is literally topsy-turvy. Only in the afterlife can we see who are the truly deserving.

The Baal Shem Tov, the eighteenth-century founder of the Hassidic movement, explained what that means through this wonderful story:

In a certain house, there dwelt two Jews and their families. One was a learned scholar, the other a poor laborer. Each day the scholar would rise from his sleep at the break of dawn and go to the synagogue where first he would study a page of Talmud. Then as the pious men of old were wont to do, he would wait a short time, direct his heart to heaven and say the morning prayers quietly and slowly, drawing out his worship until almost midday.

His neighbor, the poor laborer, also rose early and went to work—backbreaking work that strained the body and soul at once—until midday, there being no time to go to the synagogue to pray with the congregation at the proper hour.

When noon arrived, the scholar left the synagogue to return home, filled with the sense of self-satisfaction. He had busied himself with Torah and prayer and had scrupulously performed the will of his Creator. On his way from the synagogue, he would meet his neighbor, the poor laborer, hurrying to the house of worship, where he would recite the morning prayers in great haste, in anguish and regret for his tardiness. They would pass each other.

When the poor laborer passed his neighbor on the street, he would utter a mournful groan, upset that the other had already finished his study and prayer in leisure before he had even begun: "Oh my, here I am just going to *shul.* He had already finished. I didn't do it right. Ay ay ay!" Meanwhile the lips of the scholar would curl mockingly, and in his heart he would think, *Master of the World, see the difference between this creature and me. We both rise early in the morning. I rise for Torah and prayer, but he. . . .*

So the days, weeks, months and years passed. Each of the two men's lives were spent in a different fashion, one in the freedom of Torah and prayer, the other in the slavery of earning a livelihood. When from time to time their paths would cross, the scholar would smirk, and the laborer would groan.

As it must to all men, death came at last to the scholar and, shortly afterward, to his neighbor the laborer. The scholar was called before the heavenly tribunal to give an accounting of his deeds. "What have you done with the days of your years?" the voice from on high called out.

"I am thankful," replied the scholar with a firm voice, in which could be detected more than a little pride, "all my days,

I served my Creator, studying much Torah and praying with a pure heart."

"But," commented the heavenly accuser, "he always mocked his neighbor, the poor worker, when they would meet near the synagogue." The voice from on high was heard, "Bring the scales."

On one side, they put all the Torah he had learned and all the prayers he had prayed, while on the other side, they put the faint smirk that hovered over his lips each day when he met his neighbor. Behold, the weight of the smirk turned the scale to guilty.

After the case of the scholar had been completed, they brought before the heavenly tribunal the poor laborer. "What have you done with your life?" asked the voice from on high.

"All my life, I have had to work hard in order to provide for my wife and children. I did not have the time to pray with the congregation at the proper time, nor did I have the leisure to study much Torah for there were hungry mouths at home to feed," answered the laborer in shame and grief.

"But," commented the heavenly advocate, "each day, when he met his neighbor, the scholar, there issued from the depth of his soul a groan. He felt that he had not fulfilled his duties to the Lord."

Again, the scales were brought and the weight of the groan of the poor worker turned the scale to innocent.

The same point was made by the famed twelfth-century Talmudist and philosopher Moses Maimonides in the *Mishne*

Torah.[18] In his legal *magnum opus* he concludes that in God's eyes a person's good deeds and shortcomings are judged qualitatively, not quantitatively. One terrible sin may outweigh a lifetime of good deeds, or one special good deed may wipe out many sins. Only God truly knows what is in each person's heart as well as the real value of our actions.

So when God tells Moses, "I will be compassionate to whom I will be compassionate," He is saying, "I know better than you who is righteous and who is wicked, who is deserving and who is not. Don't presume to improve upon my judgment."

"And He [God] said, 'You cannot see My Presence and live.'"

What in the world does that mean?

Moses wants to "see" God, to understand God's ways. But God tells Moses, "As long as you are alive, you will never fully 'see.'" The entire picture is not visible from our limited perspective in this world.

Imagine yourself standing with your nose pressed to an impressionistic painting. In one place you see splotches of the most breathtaking royal blue, in another there is a big splotch of black, in another a splotch of white. It is not until you step a good dozen feet away that you see what the painting depicts—it's van Gogh's "Irises."

This is just as true when it comes to understanding God's plan. At times we see the colorful parts, at times the dark parts, but we can never step back far enough to see the whole picture. To step back far enough is to step into the next world.

Our existence here on Earth, and our comprehension of the real meaning of our lives, is very limited. This is God's message to Moses, the same message He gives Job when that long-suffering man asked for understanding. God says, "The facts at your disposal in the arena of life are insufficient for the kind of knowledge that you seek to possess."

IN PARTNERSHIP WITH GOD

"And the Lord said, 'Behold, there is a place alongside Me, and you shall set yourself on the rock.'"

To help Moses grasp the reasons for the presence of evil on Earth, God tells him to stand "alongside Me." This phrase echoes a similar idea from Genesis when man is first created in the image of God. Man is given a role to play in completing God's work, commensurate with his greatness. He is told that he stands as a partner alongside God up above; he is not a passive observer down below.

Why was Moses told to set himself upon a rock? Because the Hebrew word for rock, *tzur,* comes from a root that means to form, fashion or shape. The rock alludes to man's purpose on Earth. Just as God is a creator, so too is man. Indeed, man is a co-creator with God, a partner in the completion and perfection of the world.

To give man a chance to exercise this function, God has purposely left the world unfinished. It was created incomplete. That is the meaning of God resting at the end of the sixth day. God was surely not tired. "God rested" means that

He stopped in mid-work. Why? So man has the opportunity to have a hand in perfecting the world. God allows for sickness so man can play a role in inventing cures. God allows for famines so man can have a part in inventing new methods of agriculture. God allows for droughts so man can participate in bringing the world closer to its ideal state by inventing new irrigation methods and by building dams and desalinization plants.

So the evil in the world only points up the work we still have to do. Evil is a manifestation of a world that is still incomplete, waiting for man to do his part and finish the job.

"When My Glory passes by, I will put you in a cleft of the rock, and I will cover you with My Hand until I pass by. Then I will remove My Hand and you will see My Back, but My Face shall not be seen."

It is here that the most important part of the answer is given. By telling Moses that he will not be able to see His face, but only His back, God is saying that it will be impossible for Moses to understand the events as they are happening. But later, in retrospect, it might be possible to make sense of what has occurred.

While you are confronting a crisis, while you are in the eye of the storm, you will not be able to understand God's purpose or logic. But once the crisis has passed, then, looking backwards in time, it will be possible to begin to understand God's ways.

We can all name events in our lives that appeared terrible

when we experienced them, but when seen from a later perspective turned out to be good. A man is hurrying on the way to the airport. He gets a flat tire, and he panics—he knows he is going to miss the plane. He is angry at fate. At that moment, it is a terrible thing. He fixes the flat, drives like mad to the airport, but to no avail—the plane has taken off without him. An hour later, he finds out that the plane went down and crashed. So the flat tire, which he cursed a few hours before, turned out to have been a blessing.

Every time there is a plane crash, we later read about people who were almost on that flight, but who for one reason or another did not get on board. When TWA flight 800 went down, there was a highly publicized story of a woman who broke her leg and had to forego a much-anticipated vacation in Paris. She had been terribly disappointed, but now continually thanks God for her injury.

There is a memorable story told in the Talmud[19] that teaches the "principle of this, too, is for good."

The renowned first-century scholar, Rabbi Akiva, while traveling by donkey through a small village, could not find lodging at any inn. He took this in stride, assuming there was a divine purpose for his difficulties. He camped out in the woods outside of town, happy at least that he had his lantern to read by and his rooster to wake him in the morning. But in short order he is visited by more calamities—his donkey runs off, his rooster dies, and his lantern blows out. But being Rabbi Akiva, he patiently accepts his fate.

The next morning, when he goes back into town, he finds that a gang of marauders had massacred the entire population. Suddenly, he understands each and every difficulty he had faced: "Had I gotten lodging, I would have been killed. Had the lamp been on, they would have seen me. The rooster would have crowed, the donkey would have brayed. Everything that happened to me I now realize was all for the good."

THE ILLUSION OF GOOD AND BAD

When we ask the question, "Why do bad things happen to good people?" we are often making erroneous assumptions. What we perceive as "bad things" might, in fact, be the best things that could happen to them.

In a survey, most people would say that poverty, ugliness and powerlessness are bad, while wealth, beauty and power are good. Certain things we are sure of.

But ask Marilyn Monroe. She had plenty of money, was gorgeous, and her fame gave her incredible power. Yet, for her, all those things brought only misery, and she eventually committed suicide.

So you can't be so sure of what is good and what is bad. You don't know the full story. Often, you are seeing the middle part, and it might take years before the full outcome is known.

I know a multimillionaire who lost his first job as a mail clerk. Unable to find employment, he was forced to start an enterprise of his own. He now says, "It is only because I got fired that I made it."

I know of one young man who as a student was so distraught over a breakup with a girl that he became suicidal. He clearly thought that this was the worst trauma of his young life. I spent a whole night with him, talking sense to him, comforting him.

Twenty years later, I ran into this young man again. "Remember me?" he grinned.

"Sure do. You owe me a night's sleep," I said.

"I came back to tell you the end of the story," he responded. And he shared with me what had happened to him since that time. His life had been filled with blessings. He had a beautiful wife and children and was very happy. Meanwhile, the girl he considered ending his life over had become an alcoholic, and by last count had been married and divorced three times.

So ultimately, with hindsight, he realized that because of his "tragic" breakup he turned out to be much better off. Of course when he was suicidal and I tried to tell him that everything would turn out for the best, he could not listen, much less understand why it was better this way.

The *Zohar*, the chief work of the Kabbalah, the body of Jewish mysticism, comments that when God created the world He pronounced it *tov m'od*, "very good." But when we look at the world, when we study history, when we watch *World News* on CNN, we find it very hard to agree with this divine judgment.

So the *Zohar* points out that God gives us a clue in the name he chooses for the first man—Adam. In Hebrew, Adam is spelled using the same letters as the word *m'od*—mem, aleph, daled—but in different sequence: *aleph, daled, mem.* Furthermore, the *Zohar* says, Adam is an acronym standing for the three milestones of human history. *Aleph,* as the first letter of the Hebrew alphabet, represents the very beginning of the story of mankind with Adam. *Daled,* for David, represents the high point in Jewish history. *Mem* stands for *Moshiach* (Messiah), who will bring the world to its longed-for state of fulfillment.

When we finally reach that stage of history alluded to by the *mem,* the days of Messiah, we will be able look at *everything* that ever happened before throughout the course of all time, from the *aleph* of Adam through the *daled* of David, and together with God, we too will be able to proclaim that the world is not only good but indeed very good—*tov "m'od."*

As Søren Kierkegaard so powerfully put it, "Life can only be understood backward, but it must be lived forward."

IN SUMMARY

The Biblical exchange between God and Moses teaches us to beware of assumptions that are incomplete and erroneous, assumptions that lead us to question the goodness of God.

Moses says to God, in effect, "God, I want to honor you totally, but my lack of understanding of Your ways interferes. How can I honor you completely when I see good people who have it bad and bad people who have it good?"

God says, "Hold off. I question two of your premises."

"Which premises?"

"Number one, don't be so quick when you call some people good and others bad, because you don't know for sure. Number two, when you say they have it bad or they have it good, are you sure of your definitions? Are you sure you know what you are talking about? You are not positive. And you can't be positive because you can't see My face. You will only be able to see it in retrospect. In retrospect a terrible thing could be the best thing. Sometimes it will take you years to see. Sometimes you will never see, not in your days on Earth anyway."

What troubles so many people, however, are the many times when even the gift of retrospect seems to give us no greater clarity. Looking backwards at one's life can be illuminating, but it can often still leave us with many unresolved questions. What can we do then? Does it mean that we will end our lives on Earth with problems never to be resolved, injuries never to be healed, cruelties never to be explained, injustices never to be set right?

It is easy to say, "Okay, he lost his job. He will find one that he likes much better—it's not so bad." But when we are watching someone slowly dying from cancer, suffering with every breath, it is not so easy—in fact, next to impossible— to say, "This, too, is for good."

A wife says to me, "My husband got sick, he remained sick for the rest of his days, and then he died. Where is the good in that? Don't tell me to wait for the end of the story. I have seen the end of the story. He died."

Yet God tells us, "Man cannot see Me and live." We don't have the entire picture even at the time of death. Death is the gateway to the great beyond—and that very description reminds us that there is more *after* our earthly passage. What is still not clear during our finite existence, God seems to be saying, will be possible to comprehend once we are blessed with the divine perspective of eternity.

Mourners for their loved ones may have a difficult time viewing death in any positive light; for them it represents an excruciating loss. But for the deceased, death is not a problem, but rather a solution to the problem. For the person involved, death is the beginning of all the answers, as we will see next.

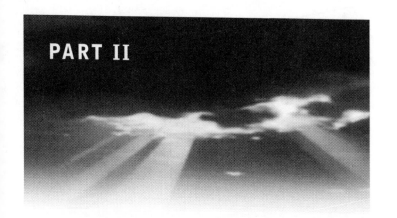

PART II

WHY WE DIE

CHAPTER 5

THE PRICE OF PARADISE

Death. The very word has been known to strike fear in the hearts of mankind.

Most of us share David's hope in the book of Psalms, "I shall not die but live and declare the works of the Lord." We agree with Woody Allen's humorous quip, "I don't want to achieve immortality through my work; I want to achieve it through not dying."

But we know that can never be. As Joshua put it on his deathbed, death is "the way of all the Earth." From the moment of birth we come ever closer to dying. Indeed, the very same God who is the Author of life is the One who has decreed the universal fate of death.

Jews pray for life. We thank God for giving us life. We begin every day with a prayer that expresses our gratitude to the Almighty for "returning our souls" so that we can continue to enjoy His world. And yet God, sooner or later, takes every one of us from it. If life is good, why did God create death? And if death is ideal, why bother with life?

To reconcile this paradox we will turn once again to the wisdom of the Talmud.

Some debates in the Talmud go on for pages and then end up with a final decision. This is because the sages realized that in later time, people would come along, suggest other arguments and say, "I bet you never thought of looking at it this way!" Therefore, the sages wanted to show that all other opinions were expressed, considered and evaluated before they were rejected.

But in this case, the final decision appears to be stated upfront. The Talmud makes a daring attempt—in contradiction to its general rules of argument—to settle the issue right at the start. It begins with a dramatic statement in answer to the question posed by the reality of death. Why do good people die? The Talmud says, "They don't."

This is what we find in Tractate Shabbat:[20] "Rav Ami said: 'I make the following statement. There is no death without sin, for it is written by the Prophet Ezekiel,[21] "The soul that sins, it shall die." There is no suffering without transgression, for it is written in the Psalms,[22] "I will smite them with a rock for their sins and with plagues for their transgressions."'"

This is a powerful declaration. Rav Ami is clearly saying that death is the result of sin. People die only because they are unworthy of life. He seems to be suggesting that anyone who dies must have committed some terrible crime, punishable by death.

THE WAGES OF SIN

To make sense of this statement we have to consider the very first sin and the first death sentence in history. How did it happen?

The Bible tells us that the first human beings were created and placed in a beautiful garden. There were a lot of trees in the garden, all of which Adam and Eve could enjoy and the fruit of which they could consume. But there were two trees that had special significance. One was the Tree of Life. The other was the Tree of Knowledge of Good and Evil, from which they were forbidden to eat lest they die. That made the latter the Tree of Death.

Human nature is such that as soon as someone says to you, "Look, you can have everything except that one thing," that one thing becomes the object of all your desires. And so, of course, that's how it turned out here as well.

Note that in the story, God says, "Of all the trees in the garden you may surely eat." He clearly says "all." It's only the Tree of Knowledge that Adam and Eve can't touch. This passage is telling us something very interesting by implication. If humans were initially allowed to eat of all trees, including the Tree of Life, then that must mean God originally intended for them to live forever. It was only when they sinned that there were consequences, among which was the edict that the Tree of Life was now placed off limits.

The story is telling us that had Adam and Eve not sinned,

they would not have known death. And neither would the world. Because of their transgression, all of us became mortal.

But I have trouble accepting that idea. I can understand Adam and Eve being subject to death because they committed the crime. But what about everybody else? What about their descendants? What about us? Why should we have to die if the original intent was that we would live forever? If this one man and his wife sinned, only they should lose their passport to eternity. But why did God take it away from everyone else as well?

Some religious traditions answer that problem by teaching that original sin is transmitted as a stain on the soul. We all share in the sin of our father, Adam. We are all guilty for his crime.

Judaism disagrees vehemently. It holds unequivocally that the soul is pure when it arrives in this world. And this is why, of course, Rav Ami was so troubled when trying to explain the problem of death. If God's original plan—the ideal in terms of God's relationship with man—is eternal life, then the only one who should die is the one who did something to warrant not being allowed to eat from the Tree of Life any longer. So for Adam, it is off limits, but for anyone else, it should not be off limits unless . . . unless what?

The only explanation for the death of future generations, according to Rav Ami, is therefore that everyone has, in one way or another, repeated the sin of Adam by disobeying God's commandments.

LIFE WITHOUT BLAME

But suppose there was somebody who did not commit a sin his entire life? If we follow Rav Ami's logic, the conclusion has to be that this person would live forever!

And, of course, the sages of the Talmud immediately challenge Rav Ami's assertion. They introduce a fanciful Midrashic tale in which the angels complain to God that Moses and his brother Aaron obeyed every commandment and still they died.

In response, Rav Ami argues that this Midrashic story is based on a false premise. Moses and Aaron were not guiltless. During their lifetimes they had in fact gone against the will of the Almighty, and that is precisely why they too had to die. In the book of Numbers[23] God says to them, "Because you did not believe in Me, therefore you shall not bring this assembly into the land which I have given you." Moses and Aaron lacked sufficient faith. Had they, however, not committed that sin, had they been perfect, they would not have died, Rav Ami insists.

But the sages of the Talmud are not easily convinced. They quote another Midrashic story. This one asserts that only four people in the history of the world died as a result of the serpent's machinations (that is, as a result of the curse pronounced upon humanity after the serpent's seduction of Adam and Eve) and not of their own guilt. These four people died even though they did nothing to warrant the sentence of death, even though they were totally guiltless. They were Benjamin, the youngest son of Jacob; Amram, the father of Moses; Jesse, the father of David; and Caleb, the son of David.[24]

The conclusion from the lives of these four seems to be that you *can* die even if you are perfect, even if you have never committed a sin. Death comes to the blameless as well as the guilty. Everybody dies.

Clearly, this is an irrefutable contradiction of Rav Ami's view. Even the innocent must die—the pure and the holy are not spared from the universal decree of death. Adam and Eve brought mortality into the world, and it is now the perpetual legacy of all their descendants.

But had we not said earlier that Judaism rejects the theory of original sin, of inheritable guilt? So how do we make sense of it all? Had not the Prophet Ezekiel said, "The son shall not bear the iniquity of the father, neither shall the father bear the iniquity of the son"?[25] Where is the justice of God when the perfect die?

The answer is profound in its very simplicity. In a perfect world, in the Garden of Eden, Adam and Eve should have lived forever. But once the world has become corrupt and is no longer a paradise because of the people in it, then everyone must die, *especially* the good people: This imperfect world is just not good enough for people who are perfect.

Faultless people now must die in order to be able to enter paradise, the place we call heaven. For them, in the words of Sir Walter Scott, "Death is not the last sleep; it is the final awakening." And this is why we can now have death without sin, not as punishment but rather as deserved reward.

THE PUZZLE OF LIFE

But wait a minute. Something still doesn't add up. We have just concluded that good people die because this bad world is not good enough for them—the good deserve a Garden of Eden, and since this world isn't paradise, they should not be here. But if that is indeed true, then shouldn't we be asking not why good people die, but rather why they live? If they don't belong on Earth, why are they here at all?

To understand the answer, we need to be aware of another basic concept of Judaism. Unlike other religions, Judaism believes that we start with a pure soul, and the whole purpose of life is to maintain it in that condition. Unfortunately, just about every person commits some transgression and tarnishes the soul they were given. For that reason, when a person dies and the soul reaches the next dimension, it must go through a purification process—in other words, it must get "dry-cleaned" somehow to bring it back to its original purity, to get rid of the stains its owner dirtied it with here on Earth.

But the obvious question is: Why bother with the trip here in the first place? Why live, if it's only going to tarnish the soul? If there is another world, and if that is an ideal existence, why not go the paradise route right from the start? The ultimate theological question about life ought to be: Is this trip really necessary?

The answer is a principle known in Hebrew as *lachmo d'kisufa*. Literally it means "bread of shame." It refers to bread that is unearned, payment that comes out of pity rather than as reward for effort. Perhaps the closest equivalent we have in English today is "welfare" when applied to people quite capable of working who choose to be "on the dole." It is the way of the parasite, and it brings with it the sobriquet of shame.

To accept welfare without even trying to work is deceitful. And that's true not only in our dealings on Earth, but also in the sight of God.

True, you could theoretically be in paradise without first making your way through life. God, in His infinite goodness, could just give you a first-class, all-expenses-paid ticket to heaven, no questions asked. But then you would know you were given a totally undeserved gift.

Judaism doesn't look favorably on the concept of a freebie. Judaism says we ought to get to heaven the old-fashioned way—we should earn it. For Jews, the only way in which the reward of ideal existence makes sense is if the person works for it. Otherwise it is a form of welfare that detracts from the self-worth of the recipient.

So this is how the whole picture makes sense. You come to Earth with a pure soul. Your mission is to do all in your power to maintain its purity. That way you can take pride in knowing that you've *earned* your place in heaven.

There is an inspiring story told about the revered eighteenth-century Rabbi Elijah Gaon (genius) of Vilna, who was found crying bitterly on his deathbed. His students couldn't understand. They knew him to be a totally just person who would surely go straight to heaven. They had studied in the Talmud, "Better is one hour in the next world than all the years on this Earth." So they couldn't understand why their Rebbe, their revered teacher, seemed reluctant to leave and was crying. "What is there to cry about, if you are leaving this place to go to heaven?" they asked.

He said, "How can I not cry when I leave a world where with a moment's effort I can still do a *mitzvah?*" He meant, of course, that there is one thing that this world has that the other world doesn't: a never-ending opportunity for growth. In heaven, things are static. It is all over.

A fanciful Hassidic tale makes the point very well:

A very rich man, who was miserly all his life and never gave any charity, dies and arrives in the next world. As he is standing in line, he hears people ahead of him being asked, "How much did you give to charity?" When his turn comes and he, too, is asked the same question, he answers: "Well, to be honest with you, I didn't give much charity, but I have my checkbook right here. I am prepared to write a check of any size, whatever it takes to get in. I am a rich man with a huge estate—any amount is not going to be a problem."

But the response comes back, "Sorry, up here we don't accept checks, only receipts."

The point, of course, is that after death there is nothing more you can do. Your opportunities for doing good deeds are all used up. And that is why the Rebbe was crying on his deathbed.

Life is good—even for the perfect person who doesn't need to be here—because it enables us to *earn* our reward, our place in paradise.

So while we have an answer to that question, others still remain. Why are some people given less time here than others? If time on Earth is so important, why is it so unequally distributed?

There are a number of possibilities, and each one of them represents a major category of Jewish thought with regard to death. We will look at seven possible answers in the coming chapter, and we'll begin with the response given when death entered the world for the very first time. Let's turn our attention to the story of Cain as he murders his brother Abel.

CHAPTER 6

THE PUZZLE
OF DEATH

Y es, some people do die, as we have seen in chapter 5, because of their sins. But, and I must stress this most forcefully, this is by no means the sole reason for death. We must remember the simple syllogism that to say that "a" can cause "b" is a far cry from saying that "b" is always caused by "a." So that while all people who commit terrible crimes will, as the Bible tells us, be punished with death, that doesn't mean that all people who die have transgressed and are being punished.

We all know the identity of the first person on Earth who died, and we know that he was blameless. The manner of his death is recorded in the Bible, in the book of Genesis. He is the second son of Adam and Eve, Abel, murdered by his older brother Cain.

There are four people on Earth, and suddenly one is eliminated. Did God want Abel dead? Did God want only three people on Earth? Does the fact that Abel died mean God decreed it?

The answer is a resounding No.

The first death is a crime committed by a murderer acting out his free will. It happened because God would not stop it. He could have, of course, but that would have meant—as we've already explained—that every action on Earth must be sanctioned by God, which would render man's free will meaningless.

So although the first death shouldn't have happened, it did. Still, God is just; therefore, we know that He must even the score and somehow make amends.

But now the question arises: How? How can God make it up to Abel? After all, Abel is dead.

Clearly, that cannot be the end of the story. Before we try to figure out its conclusion, we have to understand its beginning. So let us examine all the elements one by one.

First, we have to assume that Abel was a good man. Indeed, the Bible makes this clear. God had accepted his offering while rejecting his brother's. God loved him. So how is it that he died?

If one asks how you can explain this death, the answer is because God didn't take his life; Cain did. In chapter 3, we explained that there are bad things that happen on this Earth that are not directly the result of God's will. They happen because somebody does something wrong. And when such things happen, God must eventually react.

I know of a person whose father was mugged and killed. The father was pious, respected, the epitome of a holy man. Prayer was his passion; charity was his delight; acts of kindness were his daily currency; and study of Biblical text consumed many of his waking hours. Yet another human being who acted in an inhuman way took his life. Once again someone repeated the crime of Cain, and a just God is now responsible for righting this terrible wrong. How will He do it?

God must punish Cain, and He must make it up to Abel. The outcome of this story, which describes how God acts in such instances, teaches us an enormous amount about God's concept of justice and mercy.

JUSTICE FOR CAIN

As far as Cain is concerned, God decrees, "A wanderer you shall be on the face of the Earth." Why is this a just punishment for murder? How is this related to the concept we have introduced earlier that God's punishment is measure for measure? Shouldn't Cain's life have been taken in return?

A common explanation among Biblical commentators is that when you kill somebody, you make that person homeless. The body had served as a kind of house for the soul, and now the soul must wander without a body. So this is how Cain's punishment fits the principle of measure for measure—he must wander the Earth without a home to call his own in the same way that he doomed his brother's soul.

Another explanation sees Cain's sentence as a kind of exile. Elsewhere in the Bible,[26] we are told that when an Israelite accidentally causes the death of another, he is exiled from his home to a city of refuge where he has to undergo spiritual rehabilitation. Cain's killing of Abel could be deemed unintentional because he could not have known just how permanent the result of his actions would be. After all, he was one of the first people on Earth and hadn't witnessed the consequences of such an act. He couldn't have known from experience that when he struck Abel he would end up taking his life.

But there is still more to our understanding of the story, because God's sentencing of Cain involves two aspects. First, Cain is to wander the face of the Earth. And second, God tells Cain that he will eventually be murdered by one of his own descendents.

Why a two-part sentence? Because his was a two-part crime. There was, of course, the murder of his brother. But there was also a refusal to take responsibility for his actions. When Cain told God, "Am I my brother's keeper?" he divorced himself from his brother, as if his brother was unrelated, separate from him.

One part of his punishment—to be a wanderer—was to experience what it means to be alone, belonging to no one. And, of course, the second part of his punishment was that he had to be killed because he had killed.

However you look at it, God's sentence was indeed measure for measure, and the two-part crime received a two-part punishment.

JUSTICE FOR ABEL

But how does God render justice to poor Abel, who was cut off in the prime of life?

Seemingly, God has two ways to solve the problem.

First, the simple solution. Although Abel, like all of us, had a job to do on this Earth, he didn't have the opportunity to accomplish it. Because he was the victim who undeservedly suffered at the hands of his brother, he must immediately be admitted to heaven. He gets a free pass by virtue of being denied a chance to earn it on Earth.

Second, the more complicated solution, which we learn from the Jewish mystical tradition, the Kabbalah, is called *gilgul n'shomot,* transmigration of souls or reincarnation.

The Kabbalah teaches that anyone whose life was taken in a manner that did not accord with God's plan, anyone who should have had longer life but didn't, has to still get his divinely decreed years. Therefore, what happens to Abel? He is reborn. He gets another chance.

Sometime later, says the *Zohar,* the masterwork of Jewish mysticism, a child is born with the soul of Abel, although he is called by another name.

This had to happen because Abel wasn't able to be Abel, no pun intended. Therefore he had to be given another opportunity to fulfill his mission in the world, to earn his place in paradise.

To illustrate, the Kabbalah even identifies for us some of the transmigrations, explaining who people we recognize from Biblical stories turned out to be in another life. And so it tells us that Abel came back as Moses. And Cain also came back for a second time, as Aaron, the brother of Moses.

In this second life, they each got a chance to complete their unfinished lives. Abel, who couldn't bring to fruition his holy potential and died in purity, could now lead the Israelites out of exile, receive the Ten Commandments on Mount Sinai and become the man who met with God "face to face." And Cain, who had originally scoffed, "Am I my brother's keeper?" became just that. As Aaron, he got to atone for that earlier crime, becoming his brother's keeper, accompanying Moses to Pharaoh's palace and serving as his spokesman. To accomplish total *tikkun,* correction of his crime of implacable hatred, Cain, the first murderer, became Aaron, who would be known as the "one who loves peace and pursues peace."[27]

So the Kabbalah tells us that in a situation where death is caused by another human being, rather than being divinely decreed, God is committed to righting both wrongs: He has to do something to the one who was responsible for the crime, and he has to do something for the one who was the victim. That is His problem. God will take care of it.

What we've discussed until now is one type of death—death at the hands of another. And perhaps in our quest to understand how can God be good, just and all-powerful and yet allow good people to die, this is the easiest scenario to resolve. God is not responsible, and God will make it right. But what if God is responsible—as when a person dies of natural causes before his time or a child dies of an illness? What then?

MISSION ACCOMPLISHED

The Talmud tells us the following story.[28] A student was walking with his rabbi, and he was quite upset, upset with God. It seems that a colleague of his, a brilliant Torah scholar who was barely past twenty, had gotten very ill and died. So the student says to the rabbi: "I can't understand it. He was a good man. Don't tell me that he died early because he committed some grievous sin. I don't believe he did. So why would God take him at this age?"

The rabbi, as if ignoring his question, points into the distance, where a man is walking. "Look, what a terrible thing," the rabbi says. "There is that worker with his bags going home. It is just a little after noon, and already he is going home." The student says, "I don't understand. What is terrible about it? The man finished his job, and he is going home." And so the rabbi says to the student, "Let your own ears hear what your mouth has said. The man finished his job, and he is going home."

We learn from this story that death can mean "Mission Accomplished." A person had fulfilled his purpose in life—and whatever it may have been is between him and God—and he can now go home. Death is an end, in one way. Yet in another way, as Seneca so beautifully put it, "The day which we fear as our last is but the birthday of eternity."

The sages develop this idea at great length, offering many different Biblical sources as proof of this truth.

It is a well-established principle in the Talmud that every person is put on this Earth for a special reason. No two fingerprints are alike. No two people are alike. Every one of us is different from the rest of the entire world—or else we wouldn't have been created. The sages teach us that every individual is unique because each one of us has a special mission in life. If we were not to exist—and this is staggering to consider—the world could not exist. The world's destiny would be different today without every single person who ever lived. Every single person is an essential piece of the tapestry that God weaves to achieve His final goals for human history.

Some of the great rabbis of past ages have tried to figure out their mission in life by looking at their talents and concluding that their special gifts were meant to be the tools for achieving what God wanted of them. They would spend their lives developing their unique talents to allow them to fulfill their God-appointed tasks, so that hopefully by the time of their death they might be able to say "mission accomplished."

CUT SHORT

It is clear, however, that some people died before their time—their tasks interrupted, unfinished.

We are told in the Talmud[29] that Abraham died before his appointed time. Abraham should have lived longer than he did. He died when Jacob and Esau, his twin grandsons, reached the age of thirteen. What a seemingly cruel end to the life of such a saintly figure, the father of our faith! At the very moment his grandchildren become bar mitzvah, Abraham is taken from the world—mind you, before his appointed time—unable to further monitor their progress or derive the *naches*, the spiritual satisfaction, they would have brought to his old age! How incomprehensible. How harsh a decree. Unless, of course, you are aware of the rest of the story.

No sooner did Esau come of age than he turned away completely from the values of his family. He became a hunter, a killer not only of animals, but of the people he had robbed and the women he had raped. How hard that would have been for his grandfather to witness. Imagine Abraham weeping, "Why did I have to live to see this?" And so, indeed, he didn't! God spared him the sight of his grandson turned hoodlum. Life for Abraham would no longer have been a blessing, and so God mercifully took him before his time.

I can't help but think to myself of Jews who died in 1939 in Eastern Europe. No doubt their loved ones mourned and wondered why this or that person died before his or her time. Only in hindsight can we understand that the deceased were spared seeing the annihilation of their families and communities. And perhaps they were spared a different kind of death, a horrible death without a shred of dignity.

Interestingly enough, there is another aspect to this line of reasoning. We're told in the Bible of yet another person who died prematurely. Hanoch, the grandfather of Noah, died well before others of his generation. At that time, life expectancy was 900-plus, but Hanoch died when he was merely 365. (Of course, we don't know what these years mean when judged in light of our life spans. Perhaps before the flood, as some commentators suggest, the Earth/sun cycle was different and the measurement of years not the same as ours. Perhaps God was reluctant to apply mortality even though Adam and Eve had brought death into the world. Perhaps people had to live longer in order to populate the Earth. We don't know.)

However we understand this, Hanoch died much younger than his contemporaries. The Bible tells us, "Hanoch walked with God, and he was no longer, for God took him."[30] Ask the sages, what does that mean? "He was no longer" seems to imply a sudden, unexpected departure. And why tell us, "for God took him"? Isn't that the definition of death for everyone, not just for him? God takes all of us when He decrees that we die!

Rashi (acronym for the twelfth-century Rabbi Solomon Bar Isaac), universally accepted as the major Biblical commentator, supplies the answer. Hanoch was a good person, but God knew he could have easily been induced to turn toward evil ways. God feared for Hanoch's future. A lifetime of good behavior was threatened by ominous possibilities that God realized would soon present themselves to Hanoch. That's why God quickly took him away. God saw what he had done until then and said of this man, "I will spare him from the next challenge, which he will not be able to meet."

So God removed him before his time to save him not, as with Abraham, from *seeing* evil, but to save him from *being* evil.

I know of a woman whose son was killed in a tragic accident. He had been constantly in trouble with the law and was estranged from his family for some time. His mother grieved the loss of her son, questioning herself and God. How might his death have been prevented? Why did God take him before giving him a chance to reconcile with his family? However, when she went to remove her son's belongings from his apartment, her guilt and her questions immediately disappeared. The son's home was filled with a collection of guns, bombs and weapons. From writings he left behind, it became clear to her that he had been planning some terrible deed that would have resulted in the death of many people. God, in his mercy, had taken him from this world before he could fulfill his criminal plan. His mother thanked God for sparing her much greater grief that would have most certainly resulted had he lived.

END TO SUFFERING

In what other instances can death be seen as a blessing? When it ends a protracted illness, accompanied by terrible suffering. In a short while, we will take up the various explanations for suffering, and how a good, just and all-powerful God can allow good people to suffer, but right now we are considering those instances—with which we are all familiar—when a family breathes a sigh of relief as an elderly victim of cancer finally finds relief in death.

In this regard, the Talmud offers an illuminating story.[31] Rabbi Yehoshuah, a very holy man, was overwhelmed by what he perceived as the evil of death, and one day he fervently prayed for its removal from the world. In a short while, in a dream, his prayers were answered. He saw himself wrestling with the angel of death, and he proved victorious. He won the battle and took away the angel's sword. He then saw, in his vision, what happened next. The angel of death tried to do his job, but without his sword he was impotent. Rabbi Yehoshuah was very happy to see this, when suddenly, he heard a groan. The groan became more intense until it became a sob that shook the very foundations of the Earth. The Talmud says, Rabbi Yehoshuah asked God, "What was that noise?" God answered, "The sound you hear is the world weeping without the angel of death. You think the angel of death is only an angel of destruction. Know that the angel of death is also an angel of mercy."

The Talmud explains that death brings suffering to an end. In that way, it is a blessing, and the Earth would be much worse off without it.

DEATH AND BIRTH

The Midrash offers us another view of what life might be like without death. We read:

Simon mourned excessively for his departed friend. He was inconsolable in his grief. One night, in a vision he heard a Divine Voice say to him, "Simon, why do you grieve so much? Is not death an inevitable incident in the cycle of life? Would you change the plan of the universe and make man immortal?" Simon gathered courage and talked back. "Why not, O Lord? God can do all things. Why should there be an end to lives as wonderful as my friend's and others like him?"

And the Divine Voice replied, "So you deny the service of death to the economy of life? Very well, then. We shall set you into a world where immortality prevails and see how you like it."

Suddenly, Simon found himself looking out on a breath-taking view of a countryside. He understood that all the magnificence before him would endure forever. Nothing of it will perish. So indeed it turned out to be. Not a flower died on its stalk. Not a blossom fell from the lilac bushes. Summer gave way and autumn came, but not a leaf withered, not a tree lost its foliage. The world in its beauty had been given a kind of fixed permanence, and it shone in the self-same luster. At last, life seemed to be free from the ravages of time and circumstance, but gradually Simon felt something was missing. Nothing died in his world, but nothing was born either. He was spared the cruelties of age, but he missed the wondrous novelties of youth. His eyes tired at the beauty of flowers, constantly the same. He longed to witness the glory of new flowers unfolding. He was ready to renounce the gift of immortality when he suddenly awoke; he had been dreaming.

He brooded for a while over his strange experience, and then he said: "Oh Lord, I thank you that you have made a mortal of flesh and blood. Someone died that I might be born, and I am willing to die that there may be growth and the emergence of new life in Your world. You are the righteous judge."

Following a Jewish funeral, the mourners are required to eat a hard-boiled egg, a symbol of life, so as to be reminded of the circle of life. Some die and some are born, and in order to have birth, we must have death.

That may be reason enough to accept death. A higher level of understanding allows us to go even further. Death in a certain sense may also serve as a time for celebration.

CELEBRATING DEATH

In another Midrash[32] we are told of a philosopher who was standing by the seashore as a new ship was being launched. Everybody was very excited. Everybody was very happy at the launching ceremony. In the distance, another ship was coming back from a long and treacherous journey. The philosopher said, "You foolish people. Aren't you doing the very opposite of what you are supposed to be doing? Here, you are all excited and happy about this new ship, and you don't know what is going to happen to it. You have no idea of what it will achieve. There is another ship that has weathered the storms of the sea. It is returning, laden with treasures. It has proven itself. That is the one to whom you should be giving your attention. That is the one whose return you should be celebrating."

This is why we don't observe birthdays in Judaism, but we scrupulously commemorate *yahrzeits,* anniversaries of the death of loved ones. That is a time reserved for looking back and in retrospect remembering what the deceased had accomplished. It is then that we can rejoice that our loved one has gone to a place where he or she might be rewarded for their achievements.

Death is a journey to another destination. To know more about where we're headed is to remove the fear of the unknown. Let us, in the next chapter, share the remarkable wisdom of Judaism on what happens to us after we die.

CHAPTER 7

LIFE AFTER DEATH

Y es, there *is* life after death.

Any discussion of death dare not ignore a major Jewish belief that has today, incredibly enough, gained new believers as a result of current medical progress.

In recent years we've seen a spate of popular movies based on the theme that souls survive after death: *What Dreams May Come,* with Robin Williams; *Ghost,* with Whoopi Goldberg; *Dead Again,* with Kenneth Branagh and Emma Thompson; and, of course, the hugely successful *The Sixth Sense,* with Bruce Willis. And who doesn't remember the closing scene from one of the highest grossing movies of all time, *Titanic,* when the dying heroine is greeted on the other side by people who have died before her?

The past decades have seen popular culture embracing an idea that for the longest time found acceptance only in mystical and paranormal circles. No one could ever have dreamt that books like James Van Praagh's *Talking to Heaven* (1997) and *Reaching to Heaven* (1999) would soar to the top of the *New York Times* bestseller list, or that Brian Weiss's *Many Lives, Many Masters* (1978) would become an international bestseller translated into more than thirty languages.

What accounts for this contemporary obsession with an idea that was formerly reserved for the realm of religion? What prompted the secular world to suddenly be so receptive to the concept of an immortal soul? The answer almost assuredly lies in an incredible medical breakthrough in the 1970s that began to play a significant role in the lives of thousands of people.

Until then, death was the great unknown. William Shakespeare's *Hamlet* expressed a truth that appeared to be valid for all times: Death, he observed, is the "undiscovered country . . . from whose bourne no traveler returns." Without benefit of personal testimony from anyone who actually completed the journey, there was no way to know what lies in store for us after death. The idea of eternal life might be inimical to our faith, but it certainly couldn't count on any valid scientific confirmation. That a conscious soul survives after death had about as much rational support as the claims of a medium at a séance.

And then, thanks to increasingly sophisticated resuscitation techniques, people died—and then came back to tell us what it was like!

Granted, those who returned clearly didn't *die* in the absolute sense of the word. People who have done groundbreaking work in the field, such as doctors Elisabeth Kübler-Ross and Raymond Moody, have come up with the name NDE—"near-death experience"—to describe the phenomenon. But NDE survivors were really far more than just "near" to dying. What permits us to think of them as having been closer to "the other side" than to what we call life is the fact that they were *clinically dead*. Their brains didn't show even a flicker of activity. Their hearts had stopped beating. And there was no way for sensations to register, for sights to be recorded and for sounds to be heard. Yet these people were able to "recall" what happened in the rooms in which their bodies rested, to describe who came and went after they heard themselves pronounced dead, and even to repeat conversations that took place in the presence of their "dead" bodies in minute and accurate detail.

With which part of their nonfunctioning brains did they remember, and how could they possibly see and hear? Their physical bodies were no longer capable of performing these tasks. Small wonder almost all of those who went through an NDE experience, whether they initially were believers, die-hard skeptics, agnostics or atheists, came to an unshakable belief in the existence of a nonphysical soul that survives the death of the body.

Theologians find it ironic that the medical profession has inadvertently succeeded where countless generations of religious leaders previously failed. Modern medicine has at last given us evidence for the existence of the human soul. The very technology designed to keep the body alive at all costs has revealed that the body is secondary to a higher meaning of self. Human beings are more than bodies. We have non-physical, invisible aspects of reality that outlive our mortal "containers." At last we've come to understand what is almost certainly meant by the Bible when it tells us that we are created "in the image of God."

WHAT HAPPENS AFTER DEATH?

As more and more people began to report on their near-death experiences, the media started to take note. TV programs, magazine articles and newspaper stories gave this phenomenon significant coverage. That not only made the topic more popular and believable, but allowed for those who could bear personal witness to feel much more comfortable talking about what happened to them. Many admitted that their fear of being ridiculed had previously held them back from sharing their experiences with others, even though they considered their journey to the beyond and back the most intense, the most important and the most meaningful moments of their lives. With the international publicity following publication of Raymond Moody's *Life After Life*, celebrities like Elizabeth Taylor and Marie Osmond felt free to talk about their own close encounters with death.

Probably the most interesting aspect of near-death experiences is their almost universal similarity. Without reference to religion, race, social status, age or the value system of the individuals involved, those who were pronounced clinically dead found themselves going through most, if not all, of these stages summarized by Moody in this composite vignette:

> *A man is dying, and as he reaches the point of greatest physical distress, he hears himself pronounced dead by his doctor. He begins to hear an uncomfortable noise, a loud ringing or buzzing, and at the same time feels himself moving very rapidly through a long, dark tunnel. After this, he suddenly finds himself outside his own physical body, but still in the immediate physical environment, and he sees his own body from a distance, as though he is a spectator. He watches the resuscitation attempt from this unusual vantage point and is in a state of emotional upheaval.*
>
> *After a while he collects himself and becomes more accustomed to his odd condition. He notices that he still has a body, but one of a very different nature and with very different powers from the physical body he has left behind. Soon other things begin to happen. Others come to meet and to help him. He glimpses the spirits of relatives and friends who have already died, and a loving, warm spirit of a kind he has never encountered before—a being of light—appears before him. This being asks him a question, nonverbally, to make him evaluate his life and helps him along by showing him a panoramic instantaneous playback of the major events of his life. At some point he finds himself approaching some sort of barrier or border, apparently representing the limit between earthly life and the next life. Yet he finds that he must go back to the Earth, that the time for his death has not yet come. At this point he resists, for by now he is taken up with his experience in the afterlife and*

does not want to return. He is overwhelmed by intense feelings of joy, love and peace. Despite his attitude, though, he somehow reunites with his physical body and lives.

Later he tries to tell others, but he has trouble doing so. In the first place, he can find no human words adequate to describe these unearthly episodes. He also finds that others scoff, so he stops telling other people. Still, the experience affects his life profoundly, especially his views about death and its relationship to life.

Not one of the people who have shared this experience, upon returning to life, is ever again afraid of death.

The Western mind has difficulty dealing with themes long identified with the spiritual. Science is quick to reject what it labels as mere "anecdotal evidence." Pioneers in the field of NDE, like Moody, Kübler-Ross and a host of others, were denied scholarly acceptance for many years. But the wealth of accumulated research began to make inroads even into mainstream journals.

Dr. Melvin Morse, a Seattle pediatrician, did extensive work with children who suffered cardiac arrests and survived, and convincingly concluded that their near-death experiences weren't drug-induced, the psychological product of fear or culturally conditioned.

He described the case of one nine-year-old patient, Kate, who was resuscitated after drowning. When she revived, she described physical details of the hospital scene while she was unconscious. She told how a guide took her through a tunnel where she met her deceased grandfather. When a figure of light appeared and asked if she wanted to go back to her mother, she responded affirmatively, and the next thing she knew she woke up in her hospital bed.

Kate added matter-of-factly that during her NDE, she traveled out of body to her home. There she saw her brother playing with a G.I. Joe in a Jeep and her sister playing with a Barbie doll. She described the clothes her parents were wearing, where her father sat in the living room and what her mother was cooking. Every one of her observations was confirmed.

The American Journal of Diseases of Children, a prestigious and mainstream medical journal, published Morse's findings in 1986. Of course, many leading physicians expressed their reservations. The medical profession isn't yet prepared to say "amen" to an explanation of death that owes more to God than to Galen. But it's surely noteworthy to recognize that secular acceptance of the idea of the soul has made more progress in the last few decades than in all the preceding millennia.

SURVIVAL AFTER DEATH

What makes survival after death so hard to imagine is our inability to picture any kind of existence that markedly differs from what we know of as life. We don't even have the right words to talk about souls and their potential for feelings, for communication, for awareness and for movement. That's why those who doubt find it so hard to be convinced. How can we believe in something, they ask, that no one can possibly describe?

Jewish tradition has for many years transmitted a beautiful parable to help us deal with the idea of a world after this one. It requires a bit of an imaginative mind-stretch. But it has the power to open us up to the possibility of another realm of existence by way of analogy with a different turning point of life with which we're all already familiar.

Try to picture, the parable tells us, twins before birth resting peacefully in the womb of their mother. Their mouths closed, fed with no effort on their part through the tube entering their navels, warmed by the fluids of the embryonic sac, they feel completely at peace and secure. They can't possibly conceive of a better, more comfortable or different way of life.

Allow them now, if you will, the gift of consciousness. Assume that they are aware of their surroundings, and they begin to consider their future. They recognize changes taking place around them, feel themselves descending and start to debate what is going to happen to them.

The brothers each have strongly opposing views. One is by nature an optimist, the other a pessimist. The first is a believer, the second a skeptic.

The believer is certain that another life awaits them after they are expelled from their present home. "I can't believe," he says with assurance, "that God would have put us here for nine months, cared for us, nurtured us, and allowed us to grow and develop without any purpose. There must have been some greater plan that we still do not know. Our presence here could only have been preparation for a more glorious life to follow. It's impossible to think that all we can look forward to is total oblivion."

His brother, however, is much more of a realist. He despises wishful thinking and unsupportable expectations. For him, faith—as Marx would put it—is no more than an "opiate for the masses." "There you go," he says disdainfully to his twin, "confusing your hope with truth. The obvious fact is that everything that gives us life—the womb where we live, the cord from which we are fed, the security of our sac—is only *here*. Once we leave this place, we must die."

The believing brother again tries to make his case. He suggests that once out of the womb, they will be able to move even more freely. He talks about the possibility of other ways of getting food. He shares his dream of a kind of independence that goes beyond their present imagination. But unfortunately he cannot put it into words. Lacking any contact as yet with life as it's lived on Earth, he is stymied when his brother puts down his views as impossible and asks him to defend his ideas with concrete examples.

So the twins come ever closer to their destined meeting with birth, separated by drastically different opinions about their fate. The believer is confident he will not only survive but be even better off than he was before. The skeptic morosely awaits the collapse of his world and the coming down of the final curtain.

Suddenly, the water inside the womb bursts. There is a pushing and pounding. The twins realize they are being forced from their home. The traumatic moment is here. The believer is the first one to exit the womb. His twin brother, still inside, listens attentively for any clue from the other side. With grieving heart, he takes note of a piercing cry coming from his brother. *So I was right after all,* he tells himself. *I've just heard my poor brother's scream of death.* And at that very moment, a joyous mother and father are congratulating each other on the birth of their first child, who has just made his presence known by his cries of life.

The parable is profound because it reminds us that different kinds of existence can never be accurately described or imagined before we encounter them. An unborn child, if it had awareness, would be unable to picture life outside of the womb. So, too, we on this Earth can't fathom the meaning of a world of souls divorced from our bodies. But just because we can't really imagine it doesn't make it any less true. Leaving our body after life may very well be the birth of the soul, as leaving the womb is the birth of the body. As the sages of many faiths put it, the world is a passageway for the soul to a higher plane. And death, in the vivid metaphor of Elisabeth Kübler-Ross, is "breaking out of a cocoon and emerging as a butterfly."

DESCRIBING THE INDESCRIBABLE

Near-death experiences have proved enormously helpful for terminally ill patients and their families to come to terms with death. Many times, knowing someone who's gone through this experience or even just reading about it provided life-changing inspiration. The great fear always associated with death—the horror of facing the unknown—has become greatly mitigated by faith in an afterlife and the comforting feeling that dying may not be such a terrible experience after all.

Descriptions from those who have had an NDE force us to revise the strong negative stereotypes we've always attached to death. Those who have come back from "the other side" find it impossible to put into words the beauty of what they experienced. All they can share with us, as this example from *Beyond the Light: Files of Near-Death Experiences* by Marisa St. Clair, clearly demonstrates, is a small measure of the bliss they enjoyed far beyond any happiness imaginable on this Earth:

> *I believe I died and went to heaven, but it wasn't my time, so I was sent back. There are no words to do justice to what happened to me. It was a hundred times more exciting than even waiting for Christmas when you're a tiny child, more exhilarating than driving the fastest car or having the best sex. I had entered into a world that had a sort of flavor of ecstasy. All colors were brighter than anything you can imagine, all the sights and sounds somehow geared to being blissful. It was like being in love a million times over. I met a being who could have*

> been God, and I was content just to be around him, but that
> wasn't to be. I remember actually sobbing my heart out when
> he told me I had to go back. I begged like I'd never begged
> before to be allowed to stay, but suddenly with a sort of loud
> click I was back in my body feeling awful. I was utterly miser-
> able for days, because I was back in this dreadful, heavy, gray
> and dull world when I could have been dead. That's a joke,
> isn't it—the idea that being dead is terrifying. If I had a choice
> right now, I'd choose death over life any time.

These are the words of Joe, a British man who had an NDE. While his conclusion sounds almost suicidal, it really shouldn't be. Together with those who shared his experience, he realized that the divine decision to send him back meant he had an obligation to fulfill an as-yet-unfinished mission. What he chose to express, though, was his newfound belief that what was waiting for him at the end of his days should be eagerly anticipated rather than fearfully expected.

Dr. Melvin Morse writes that his research convinced him that by dying we become "more alive, more fulfilled and blissfully happy." He's sure he'll get the chance someday himself to verify what one little girl said to him after her near-death experience: "Heaven's fun. You'll see!"

Hopefully all of us, too, will be able to come to the same conclusion when we complete our final journey. Then all of our problems about God's "cruelty" for causing death will instantly vanish in the realization that, in the words of Robin Williams, "Death is nature's way of saying, 'Your table's ready.'"

CHAPTER 8

WHEN A CHILD DIES

S o far we have established that, according to Jewish sources as well as a significant number of contemporary authorities, death is a knock on the door with the message: "It is time to leave the party here to go elsewhere." If we can agree that the dying person is merely being called someplace else—to another party, which is far better than this one—then death is not so much of a problem.

When we asked the question—What is the purpose of the prior years spent on this Earth, the purpose of life?—we concluded it is to spiritually perfect ourselves. We do not want a freebie; we do not want to be party crashers. We want to have earned our invitation. We want to complete the task assigned to us here on Earth.

But what are we to think when a person clearly has not completed his mission, when a person leaves this Earth before he could possibly have achieved anything? When people die young, it surely cannot be said that they fulfilled their life's purpose. If they died as a result of a violent act of another, we were able to explain that an all-powerful God chose not to interfere with the free will of the perpetrator. But what are we to make of the death of a little child from an incurable disease or an unknown cause? What are we to say then?

A BORROWED TREASURE

One important insight the Midrash[33] asks us to consider is the story of the second-century rabbinic great, Meir, and his wife Bruria.

One Sabbath, while the famed scholar was in the synagogue, both of his young sons died suddenly, with no explanation. Their grieving mother covered their bodies with shrouds and closed the door of the room where they were lying. When her husband returned home and asked the whereabouts of the sons, she instead asked him to recite the *havdalah* prayers that conclude the Sabbath. After he did so, she asked him, "As a great rabbi and teacher, will you give me an answer to a legal question?"

"What is your question?" he asked.

"Some years ago, a person of importance gave me two precious jewels to watch over. Now he has come to claim them. Must I give them back or not?"

Surprised by the simplicity of the question, the rabbi replied without hesitation, "How can you ask such a thing? Of course, if you have someone else's property, you must return it."

She then took him by the hand and led him to the room where the bodies of the boys were lying. She removed the shrouds, and he saw his dead sons. Immediately, he began to weep. But she said to him, "My dear husband, did you not say that we should return the property to its owner? The Good Lord has given, and the Good Lord has taken away."

The Talmud reminds us that our children are not our possessions. They are God's creations and God's gifts. Sometimes He asks for them back when we still would like to keep them.

But any parents who have lost a child and known the excruciating pain of such a loss would still have to wonder why this experience was visited on them. Why had they been singled out for such suffering?

Clearly, we are back to the original dilemma of Job—is God good? Would a good God do something so cruel? Yet Bruria remained firm in her faith. She called God the Good "Lord." She used the name that refers to the Almighty in His mode of kindness and compassion.

How was she able to do that? Because she understood that the very same God who now took these lives had been magnanimous in bestowing such a precious gift in the first place. When the Lord had given, everyone acknowledged God's kindness; now that He has taken, can I possibly condemn the One who had previously shown Himself so desirous of showing me good? No. This is an act incomprehensible to me, but it comes from the hands of someone who will never do me harm.

THE PURPOSE OF AN INFANT'S LIFE

Yes, there is comfort in knowing that God gave us the gift of a child in the first place, and it is He who asks for its return. Yes, there is consolation in believing that an even better world awaits the soul of someone who ascends to a higher plane of existence. But the question begs to be asked: What purpose could possibly have been served by a life of such short duration? If all of us have a mission, what was the mission of the infant that God took from us soon after birth?

The first possible answer we will examine is perhaps the hardest to accept and requires the greatest care in its analysis.

When an infant dies, it cannot be said that he has suffered much. His tiny life was so pitifully short that he was almost certainly unaware of either his life or his death. Our problem is not with his pain, but with his purpose. What was his soul supposed to accomplish on Earth?

The remarkable answer may be that the infant's mission on Earth was fulfilled *by his life and immediate death*. His mission may have been to be the vehicle for—and I am sorry that I have no better way to say it—a repayment of his parents' debt to God. Not, of course, that God requires repayment; it is the repayment of a debt that is necessary to help the parents grow intellectually, emotionally and spiritually. It may seem like a tough pill to swallow, but growth is why we are here, and when it is arrested, God steps in to urge the person forward. A tragic and traumatic message may well be the wake-up call people need to make them reconsider their values and their approach to life.

The Midrash[34] offers us this parable. A man has borrowed heavily from the king and has no means of paying the money back. The king has repeatedly sent a messenger to collect the debt, but each time the man has begged off. Finally, the king does a strange thing. He arranges for the very sum the man owes to be thrown through the window into the man's house. The man rejoices at the unexpected treasure. Shortly thereafter, the king's messenger arrives to collect the debt once more. And now the man must part with his newfound fortune in order to finally resolve his account with the king.

A puzzling story. The king has given very generously to the man. But the man cannot pay back what he owes. So the king in his great magnificence makes him an anonymous gift to allow him to make good on the outstanding debt!

Within this riddle lies a concept that describes one of God's dealings with us, servants of the King of Kings. When a man commits a transgression for which he deserves death, God does not collect immediately. He waits until the man is married, and he makes him a gift of a child. Then God takes the infant away from him. What has occurred? This man has paid up his debt, and God has retrieved what is His.

Gershon Winkler[35] explains this idea in a powerful and moving manner: "In the above Talmudic allegory, the king's concern was not to fill his treasury. (After all, he secretly gave the debtor the means to pay him back from his own treasury.)

The sole purpose was that the borrower clear his account. For as long as the account is delinquent, the relationship is obstructed. God does not wish to take a person's child away as some kind of offering or appeasement, neither of which God needs. Rather, the divine intent is to provide the parents with the opportunity to refocus their reference point of reality. It is as if God is saying, "This world is not yours. It is mine. All that you perceive as your own came from Me, including yourself. I took back the child I gave you because your child is but an extension of yourself. I do not need what I take nor do I delight in your suffering after I have taken. Rather, I only wish to clear your account whose delinquency has created an expanding gap in our relationship. Now I have taken back what was mine, and you have paid your debt by your anguish. I can only hope that you utilize the experience to heighten your spiritual perspective."

A CLEAR MESSAGE

The Bible and Midrash abound with illustrations of this type.

We are told that Judah, who had sold his brother Joseph into slavery, atoned in this manner for the pain he caused his father Jacob. Judah had lied to his father when he claimed that wild animals had killed Jacob's most beloved son, Joseph. The old man's grief knew no bounds.

Seeing Jacob's anguish, God tells Judah: "You have not had any children until now. You do not understand the torment of losing a child. I make you this oath. You shall now marry a woman and bury your child, and then you will know. Then you will understand the intense pain you caused to your father."

Thus Judah experienced God's justice according to the principle of measure for measure. He learned the degree of hurt he had inflicted on his father. There is no denying that there is an educative process that comes about through the loss of a child. As Winkler put it, "It refocuses your sense of reality."

People whose lives have been centered on totally false values find themselves brought up short when they have to face tragedy for the first time. One man said to me that a terrible loss in his life caused him to reevaluate his attitude to his family. He put it simply: "I grew up."

Mike Wallace of *60 Minutes* fame once confessed on television that the death of his son proved the single most mind-altering experience of his life. It caused him to review his life, his purpose on Earth, his priorities. Everything he is today, he said, is due to the transformation he experienced in the wake of this tragedy.

Sometimes, of course, the reaction to the death of a child is just the opposite. Instead of learning from the experience, people can grow bitter, try to drown their sorrows in alcohol or abandon previous values they might have held. A moment when God addresses anyone as directly as this is filled with spiritual potential, and the person can respond positively or negatively in accordance with his free will. Choosing to learn something that improves the quality of one's life after tragedy, however, allows us to see how we can emerge from darkness to light; it turns an otherwise meaningless calamity into a meaningful message.

THE MESSAGE FOR OTHERS

Tragedies may have meaning not only for those who directly suffer their blows. They may well be part of a larger plan to inspire and to educate a far greater circle of witnesses.

Anyone observing grieving parents is also educated by extension. As a rabbi, I have heard people visiting a house of mourning often tell me: "I suddenly realize that I am so lucky! I have to run home and kiss my children. I have been taking my blessings for granted. Now I realize how fortunate I am."

If you lose something, aren't you all the more appreciative of what you have? If a woman has a miscarriage and then gives birth to a healthy child, isn't she more grateful for the gift granted her? If a mother had a child who died, won't she be all the more appreciative of the other children she will later have?

As much as we might not like to hear that there is an educational purpose to a terrible tragedy, life proves again and again that it is so. Loss or near loss helps us to put into perspective what we have and what we value as important.

I read an article a while back by a father, a writer, whose child had been diagnosed with cancer of the eye. A religious man, he had written the article as a kind of open letter to his community, to answer the question he had been often asked since the terrible news became known, whether this challenge had shaken his faith in God. He wrote, "This crisis in my life from which I have learned so much reassures me that God cares." He went on to explain:

Those qualities I had previously thought most precious and important—my intelligence, ambition and creativity—were completely unimportant to me in my crisis, useless to help Yael [the afflicted baby] or even to help myself. It was unimportant whether I was cultured or well read, or whether my friends were interesting or famous. It didn't matter whether I knew more or less than others, and whether they or I were more successful. I realized how often I had failed others through preoccupation with my own talent, so much less important than my ability to care.

These simple lessons seem to me so important, so to the heart of life, that I have come to embrace my own pain with a kind of tenderness. I think through it I may have gained what is best about myself.

Could I have learned these things on my own in a less traumatic way? Some people do, and I suppose I might have also, but I didn't. I am not bitter, but rather reassured that God cares because he interrupted my life to ensure I learned lessons I couldn't live without.[36]

SINS OF THE FATHERS?

There are lessons for the parents in the death of the child. But what about the soul of the child? Was there any intrinsic value in its short life aside from its effect upon others? Is its death a punishment of some sort? But it had not lived long enough to transgress! Can it be that it is being punished for some sin of its parents?

I am often asked about a puzzling sentence in the Ten Commandments that seems to imply this is true: "I am the Lord Your God, who visits the sins of the fathers onto the children to the third and fourth generation."

Let me set the record straight. This often mistranslated and misunderstood sentence does *not* mean that punishment for sins of the parents are transferred onto the children. If that were true, we would be back to the dilemma of Job, asking how a just God could do such a thing. In many places in the Bible[37] we are assured that this is not true. Indeed, we are repeatedly and explicitly told that God never punishes the children for their parents' sins.

The more logical interpretation of this sentence does not translate the words *poked avon avot* as "who *visits* the sins of the fathers." Far better, and in accord with the positive implication this word usually has in the Torah, is to translate it "who *remembers*" or "who *takes into account* the sins of the fathers." What it teaches us is that God doesn't simply judge children for their actions without taking note of how badly their parents may have raised them and what they failed to teach them. Children whose parents neglected to teach them honesty will not be judged as harshly when they steal as children who were taught to be honest but stole nevertheless. Children who never were taught the sanctity of the Sabbath will not be punished for a lack of observance rooted in ignorance rather than rebelliousness. God takes all social and environmental factors into account when deciding the extent of a person's liability.

But for our purposes here, another interpretation—a more profound and mystical one—is of even greater interest. According to the Kabbalah, there is great significance to the last phrase, "unto the third and fourth generation." God remembers an individual's sins through three and four generations as He sends *that very same soul* back to Earth— through reincarnation—to atone for past sins. Indeed, that rectification process might take three and four generations to accomplish.

The Kabbalah says that an infant who dies had to come back for a short period of time to complete a minimal task. The parents have fulfilled a commandment to "be fruitful and multiply" and been afforded an opportunity to express a high level of love. And the infant, even without performing a conscious act, could have brought about a change in others by allowing them the opportunity to demonstrate love. That may have been all that was needed for it to complete its last cycle of atonement. More, once it died, it could have been given credit by God for the meritorious works the parents undertook in its name.

A number of foundations have been created to fight diseases and do charitable works in the name of children who died young. Kirk Douglas, for example, built a playground for the impoverished Arab children of Jerusalem and dedicated it in memory of the tiny children who were present in the day-care center of the Alfred P. Murrah Federal Building in Oklahoma City when it was destroyed by a terrorist's bomb. Douglas said, "It seemed to me fitting to dedicate a playground in the memory of the Oklahoma children in the Holy City of Jerusalem where children are no strangers to terrorists' bombs."

Thus the deaths of these children accomplished much good and caused the outpouring of much love, and perhaps that was why they came to Earth for such a brief period of time— seemingly merely to die.

But is that also the reason little children suffer? Here we come, at last, to the most difficult segment of our examination—the reasons for seemingly pointless suffering. This we will take up in the very next chapter.

CHAPTER 9

THE GIFTS OF AGING, PAIN AND ILLNESS

A sk people to tell you what they think is good about old age and the only thing most of them will be able to come up with is that, as Maurice Chevalier said, "It beats the alternative." The reality is that aging brings our youthfulness to an end. It carries with it the burden of disabilities. It mocks our former strength and gives the lie to our previous beauty. For many, if not most, people, Edith Wharton was right: "There's no such thing as old age; there is only sorrow."

Ask people to tell you what they think is good about pain and suffering and they'll look at you as if you're crazy. Maybe the famous observation of William Hazlitt is a little too severe. "The least pain in our little finger," he said, "gives us more concern and uneasiness than the destruction of millions of our fellow-beings." But pain surely seems something to be avoided at all cost. Julius Caesar came to the conclusion, "It is easier to find men who will volunteer to die than to find those who are willing to endure pain with patience."

And finally, ask people to tell you what they think is good about a final illness and they'll probably tell you what so many have said they pray for: "When it's my time to go, please let it not be drawn out; please let me die peacefully in my sleep so I can be spared the anxiety and the fear of knowing that death is near."

To put it bluntly, aging, pain and a final lingering illness are commonly considered three major curses.

But according to the Jewish tradition, each one of these three came to the world as *God's response to a human request.* Three very important people, the three patriarchs, felt it was crucial for them to age, to suffer and to know the imminence of death, and God simply couldn't turn them down. Far from being three curses, aging was God's blessing to Abraham; suffering was the gift that was granted to Isaac; a critical illness was the Lord's positive reply to Jacob's appeal.

How can that possibly be? And what is the Biblical source for such a seemingly far-out commentary? To appreciate what the rabbis said, you have to know a principle of Torah analysis.

To the sages of the Talmud, a "first" appearance in the Bible is incredibly significant. It means that what it describes *hasn't ever happened before.* The Talmud[38] takes note of the occasions when the Bible makes reference *for the very first time* to the presence of old age, suffering and illness in the world. Clearly, the author of this text—God—means to send a strong message. And what could that message be? That what is now mentioned didn't exist before then and only made its appearance in light of the context of this story. From this, the Talmud proceeds to arrive at three remarkable conclusions.

Old age appears for the first time in reference to Abraham. Suffering appears for the first time in reference to Isaac. And illness appears for the first time in reference to Jacob.

The Talmud impresses this fact on us and then offers us this intriguing Midrash.[39] It relates that the three patriarchs—Abraham, Isaac and Jacob—each *asked* God for a favor. In each case God fulfilled the request and granted a "gift."

Could that be correct? The three worst scourges of mankind are, in fact, three gifts? And they came into the world because the wise patriarchs—the wisest of men, we are taught—asked for them? We must be missing something when we think of old age, suffering and illness as curses instead of blessings.

To understand what the sages had in mind, let us take a closer look at these stories.

THE GIFT OF OLD AGE

Abraham is the first person to ask God for old age. He said to God, according to the Midrash, "Master of the universe, if there is no such thing as old age, a man and his son will enter a place and the people there will not know who deserves more honor. They will look the same. There will be no difference between an immature child and the mature man who has acquired a certain level of intelligence, experience and wisdom. That is not good. If you will be so kind, crown us with old age. Put a little white in the hair, make a person look a little bit older, more distinguished. Then others will know to whom to give greater respect."

The Midrash goes on to relate that upon hearing his request, God said to Abraham, "A good thing have you asked for. And from you it shall begin."

Abraham recognized that there is a benefit to old age. God didn't give this "gift" until Abraham asked for it because it was not until then that humanity had reached the necessary level of wisdom to accept and understand the blessing to be found in aging.

Therefore, it is written in the Bible in Genesis,[40] "And Abraham was old, advanced in days." That is the first time the word "old," *zikna,* makes its appearance in the Biblical text.

I stress here that Abraham asked for and received the "benefit" of aging. He did not ask, nor receive, the *disabilities* of old age. That came later. At this point we are concentrating on the positive sides to the white hairs and wrinkled brow. They are signs that allow the world to recognize a person with experience and wisdom—that someone precious and special is in their midst. Cultures that respect only the young choose strength over knowledge, power over profundity. What

Abraham brought to the world as a result of his wish being fulfilled is the awareness that age deserves to be honored for those ways in which it is superior to youth. Abraham didn't want to be confused with being just "one of the boys"; he preferred to look his age so that his opinions are accorded the deference due to experience.

THE GIFT OF SUFFERING

The Midrash continues: Some years later, Isaac was the first to ask God for suffering. Before Isaac, the only Biblical instances of suffering are by way of punishments.

As the Midrash continues its exploration of "firsts" in the Bible, it fills in the story this way: Isaac said to God, "Master of the Universe, if a person were to die without having borne any affliction, he will arrive in the next world with a tremendous debt to pay. After all, nobody is perfect, and everyone will have to atone in some way for his or her sins and errors. I am afraid to face You, never having suffered any hardship on this Earth. I pray, let me assume some of it now, so it will diminish the balance that I will surely have to pay later in the next world. Please, God, let me have some of it here."

To this request, God replies, "A good thing you have asked for. And from you, it shall begin."

So for the first time an affliction—in this case, blindness—appears.[41] And that is why it is written, "When Isaac grew old, his eyes became weak from seeing, and he became blind."

THE GIFT OF FINAL ILLNESS

And then, the Midrash tells us, some years later, Jacob asked for illness. He said to God, "Master of the Universe, people are dying without warning. Their breath is taken from them, and they are gone in an instant. They sneeze, and they are dead." (Have you ever wondered why in every language and culture we wish a person who sneezes good health?) "When people die suddenly they don't have a chance to settle their affairs, to make peace with those they have wronged, to ask forgiveness of God and fellow man. I want to know when I am going to die—two or three days before my time. Please, God, give me the gift of a final illness before I am cut down by the angel of death."

To this request, too, God replies, "A good thing you have asked for. And from you, it shall begin."

So in Genesis,[42] we first find the word for serious illness, *choleh*. A messenger comes to Joseph to tell him, "Behold, your father is ill." And shortly thereafter Jacob dies, but not before he has the opportunity to bid a final farewell to his family.

WHY THESE THREE "BLESSINGS"?

The sages of the Talmud also teach us that each of the three patriarchs personified and served as the paradigm of an important *middah,* a crucial character trait: Abraham was the epitome of kindness; Isaac demonstrated strength; Jacob represented truth, which is necessary to determine the proper balance between kindness and strength.

With this in mind, we can better understand the significance of each one of their requests to God. Because of their specific natures, each one of them required just the particular "blessing" that the Midrash discovered in their stories. Precisely because of who they were, they could, respectively, see value in old age, suffering and illness.

Abraham, the paragon of kindness, was granted old age, because it is old age that allows the passion of youth to cool, a fiery temper to be calmed, anger to dissipate. It is old age that permits kindness to fully bloom and find expression. The old no longer need to fight for their place in the sun. The wisdom of years permits kindness full reign.

Isaac, the epitome of strength, asked for suffering because in the presence of suffering we are first witness to the awesome power within us. Don't we often allude to this truth when we say, "What doesn't kill you makes you stronger"? Isaac might never have known what he was capable of were he not put to the supreme test of being offered by his father for a sacrifice. So, too, many people find their true fortitude when they first need it, when life tests them in an unforeseen way and they measure up to the crisis.

Jacob, who was known for truth, a balance between kindness and strength, asked for a final illness because it is balance that we best discover when we know the end of our days on Earth is near. Extremes are the result of our inability to grasp the full picture. But the closer we stand to death, the more clearly we see the real meaning of our goals, values, ambitions and strivings. Knowing our days are numbered gives us the wisdom implicit in the "balance principle."

KNOWING WHEN DEATH IS NEAR

Of the three "gifts" that we normally consider curses, the gift of aging to Abraham is probably the easiest one to grasp in a positive sense. We can understand that, aside from its problems, aging still offers many wonderful rewards. Robert Browning wasn't totally wrong when he advised us, "Grow old along with me, the best is yet to be." Wrinkles, after all, may be badges of honor testifying to our maturity. It's not that the young don't have them as much as that they don't yet deserve them.

The "gift" of Isaac is the one that gives us the greatest difficulty. No matter how much we try to rationalize it, pain and suffering still seem too cruel to be acceptable as a God-ordained condition. That's why we're going to leave a fuller discussion of this crucial problem to the next section of this book. It's important enough to deserve a more extended analysis.

What I do want to clarify more fully before we conclude this chapter is the "gift" asked for by Jacob. Imagine: Jacob could have departed from this world in the same way as all of his contemporaries. According to the Midrash, everyone whose time was up was suddenly seized by a sneeze . . . and was gone. Sounds great to me. Not a moment of worry. No stress, no anxiety. Not even the sad scene of a family sitting close to the deathbed, tearfully coming to terms with a discernably imminent tragedy. What could Jacob have been thinking? What did he see as the benefit of his desire for a last and final illness?

It's clear that Jacob wanted it because it has a benefit. What is the benefit? What is the gift? The gift, in one word, is awareness—knowing that it is really going to happen.

When, as a young rabbi, I would be called to the bedside of a dying person, I would often ask the family, "Does the patient know that he is going to die?" Sometimes the family said yes; sometimes the family said no. But then, if I had the opportunity to speak to that person, invariably I would learn that he knew the truth, although he preferred not to discuss it with the family. It was as if both sides were playing a game— the family wouldn't want to discuss death with the sick person so as not to upset him, and the patient wouldn't want to discuss it with the family so as not to frighten them.

I would even go further and say that the closer death was, the more keen the awareness of the one dying that it was imminent.

What does such awareness accomplish? Why does this seem to be a divinely implanted premonition? First, it allows you to "prepare to meet your Maker." How do you prepare? Clearly, no need to pack your bags. But there is an opportunity to unload your bags, if you will. The sages teach us that appropriate, sincere repentance can undo a lifetime of transgression. They teach us that there is opportunity to make amends for sins against God and for sins against other people, which only they can forgive here on Earth. There is time in these last moments before death to rectify many things that might have gone uncorrected if the person had died suddenly. So awareness has significant benefit for a dying person. But it also has significant benefits for the survivors.

In the case of Jacob, all his sons are called to his bedside, and he blesses each one. The blessings are odd in their phrasing. Jacob doesn't say, "You should have a good life" and "You should accomplish this or that." Jacob's blessings are actually exhortations. They are instructions. In some cases they are even critiques. At first glance, one might ask, why are they then called blessings? Jacob is telling his sons off!

But the truth is that he is doing it for their own good, in their own best interest. He is pointing out their character flaws only so they have a better understanding of their failings. He tells each one, "This is your challenge on Earth, and this is what you need to work on."

Why didn't he do this earlier? one might ask. It is possible that he wasn't ready to say it until then, but there also could be a deeper meaning here: Perhaps his sons weren't ready to hear it.

Many times I have had people say to me, "My father said this to me on his last day . . . ," or "My mother asked me to do this and this. . . ." Is there a person who wouldn't do something that a parent asked her to do at the very end of life? Such requests carry tremendous weight and validity.

A congregant in my synagogue, who made a rare appearance on the High Holidays only, suddenly started appearing for services every Sabbath. I couldn't help myself and asked him what caused this spiritual awakening. "Rabbi," he said to me, "on his deathbed, my father said to me, 'It would mean so much to me if you found your way back to the synagogue.' So showing up here every week is the least I can do for his memory."

Another man I know, a very wealthy individual who was not known for philanthropy, suddenly endowed several major institutions with considerable gifts. Why? "Because my mother, before she died, begged me to help others with some of the great gifts God has bestowed on me."

The Talmud[43] teaches that it is a commandment to fulfill the wishes of a dying person. The words of the dying are considered to carry much more power. There are exceptions, of course—a dying parent cannot command his child to sin or marry someone against his wishes. But in general, the dying person is given the authority by God to leave an indelible mark on those who spend the last moments with him or her.

It is true, of course, that the benefits we spoke of can be accomplished with a terminal illness of short duration. Surely the lasting good that can come about as a result of an anticipated farewell could just as well be achieved from a sickness of days rather than months or years. How can we deal with the suffering that never seems to end?

It is Isaac's "gift" that has troubled mankind the most. Pain and suffering don't allow for facile explanation. Isaac may have not only understood, but even gone so far as to desire what is almost universally feared. But we still see his blindness as curse. We find it almost impossible to accept. And yes, unlike Isaac, we are tempted to turn to God and implore him to take back his "gift" and restore us to a world without suffering. More than anything else, our faith in a good God is challenged by the world's screams of pain. That is what we are going to deal with in the pages to come.

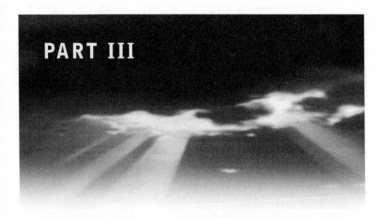

PART III

WHY WE SUFFER

WHY WE SUFFER

CHAPTER 10

MAKING SENSE OF SUFFERING

Here is a bitter truth: We only die once; we can suffer endlessly.

Death can be defended, as the Hassidic Rabbi Mendel of Kotzk put it, because, "Death is just a matter of going from one room to another, ultimately to the most beautiful room." Suffering, however, seems to lack any justification. Doesn't God hear when we scream out in pain? Or doesn't He care? Is it possible that we feel compassion when we watch our friends' anguish, yet the All-Merciful Lord can look away and ignore the pleas of the afflicted?

Suffering, more than anything else, jeopardizes our faith.

It is often heartbreaking to hear the plaintive tone in the voices of some people when they express their anguish. More troubling even perhaps than the actual pain is its apparent pointlessness. "I just want God to tell me that there is a why, that it is not meaningless, that it is not in vain," they cry to me.

Nietzsche was right: "What really raises one's indignation against suffering is not suffering intrinsically, but the sense-lessness of suffering."

A person can endure almost anything if he knows that it is for a reason. We can put up with the pain of an operation if the doctor tells us: "Be strong now. This is going to hurt for a while, but I am going to remove that tumor and after you heal, you will see how much better your life will be from now on." Then we can respond: "Okay, if there is a benefit to all this, I will endure that pain. I will grit my teeth, and I will say, 'I am getting something out of it.'"

But if pain has no purpose, if suffering visits us on some random-selection basis, then it can only bring us closer to despair.

Living in a world filled with incurable diseases and cancers, we know, realistically, that suffering can't be eliminated, but we also innately feel that it can be made tolerable through the anesthesia of understanding.

To begin to understand the purpose of pain and suffering as Judaism explains it, we will again turn to the pages of the Talmud.

In this and subsequent chapters, we will examine some of the most powerful answers in Jewish tradition to the very complex problem of human suffering. We must bear in mind at all times as we review these different responses that our finite minds, of necessity, are limited in grasping truths of infinite scope. In addition, there is never only one explanation that can solve all our difficulties. If our own actions are pregnant with multiple layers of meaning, can we expect less from God?

Therefore, in our search for answers we must acknowledge not just one possibility, but rather an amalgam of possibilities. And of these there will be some solutions we can readily understand, as well as others, more complex, imbued with subtle layers of profound significance, which we have yet to fully comprehend.

THE REBUKE PRINCIPLE

> *My child, do not reject the correction of the Lord;*
> *Do not despise His rebuke.*
> *For whom the Lord loves, He rebukes,*
> *Like a father who favors the child.*[44]

This famous quotation from Solomon's book of Proverbs gives us the first answer to our question: Why do the good suffer? I call it the "rebuke principle."

The rebuke principle posits that God inflicts some forms of pain on us out of love for the purpose of discipline, for our own good. And whereas we might be inclined to respond to this explanation for suffering with, "God, do me a favor, don't be so good to me," there is considerable evidence in Biblical and Talmudic texts that, at times, this is the very purpose that God seems to have in mind when pain visits us.

At the outset let me say that I am not making an argument here that a father would discipline his child by giving him or her cancer or AIDS. There are clearly some degrees of suffering that would be outside this principle. Having said that, let us see where it might apply.

Note that the verse from Proverbs begins with "My child." This is very important because it sets the tone for the message that follows. The advice is not from a teacher or a stranger, but from someone much more intimate—a father. "For whom the Lord loves, he rebukes, like a father. . . ."

Of course, children who hear their parents say, "I am doing this for your own good" tend not to believe it. When you are young and lacking in wisdom, you are inclined to think that you should be allowed to do whatever you want to do. Stay out past midnight. Go to a drinking party. And your parents say, "No, for your own good you will stay at home and do your homework."

You argue and pout, cry, get angry, slam the door. But when the other kids get into a car wreck because they have been drinking, or when all that homework has paid off with an admission to Yale, well, you see how it might have been good for you after all.

At the time when the discipline was administered, you didn't appreciate it because you lacked the maturity to see the whole picture. It seemed arbitrary and cruel to you then, just as God's correction seems to you now!

Likewise, when a small child, three years old, who had been told never to cross the street without an adult, runs out into traffic, the parent does not immediately begin a half-hour speech on the dangers of fast-moving cars. The parents spank the child, hoping to deliver the sharp and clear message, "Don't ever do this again!"

Is it cruel? Yes, any form of corporal punishment has some degree of cruelty in it, and this is why it is controversial. Yet studies show that there is no sharper way to deliver a message. Later, you can reason with the child, explain, "It hurts me more than it hurts you." The child won't really believe you— your statement seems illogical to him. But you know it is true. And, of course, this is the one phrase that has been transmitted from generation to generation—what children reject as parental absurdity becomes their own maxim when they themselves are faced with the task of raising their children!

We can translate this idea, image-wise, into our relationship with God. Let us say that God is the parent and we are the three-year-old child. We respond to a painful experience in our lives by saying to God, our parent, "This doesn't make sense. Why are you doing this to me?" The parent answers: "Look, I am going to try to explain it to you, but you probably won't understand it yet at your age. But someday, when you grow up a bit, you *will* understand that this was for your own good."

The image of parent-child relationship—a wise, all-knowing father and uncomprehending little child—is what the Bible wants to convey in its instruction that, "For whom the Lord loves, He rebukes, like a father who favors the child."

Now when we ask, "Why do the wicked prosper and the righteous suffer?" we can respond with the insight we've gained from this verse. Yes, it's precisely because they are loved by God that they suffer.

In his famous work *The Guide to the Perplexed,* Maimonides argues that the closer you are to God, the more in touch you are with Him, the more correction there is likely to be. When God sees your love for Him, He returns it in *very same measure.* It's then that He seeks to guide you at every step. Out of His extra measure of concern and His caring love, He corrects you so that you can be the best that you can be.

A person who is not interested in God will find that God is likewise not so interested in him. God leaves him alone, but while that might feel good at first, eventually it ends up feeling very bad. It feels good to a teenager not to be supervised by his parents. He can cut school anytime he wants, stay up to all hours of the night, sample drugs or alcohol or worse. It doesn't feel so good to that teenager when he ends up jobless, an alcoholic or in jail. It might have hurt some to get the loving guidance and correction from a parent, but wouldn't it have been worth it in the long run?

As I write this, I have in front of me a powerful ad put out by the anti-drug campaign. It is a full-page picture of a seemingly angry teenager. Written over him in huge bold letters are the words **GET OFF** at the beginning of the paragraph and **MY BACK** at the end. In smaller print are squeezed in the boy's thoughts as he seems to scream his defiance: *Okay, it may seem like I hate my parents, but I'm really demonstrating what a therapist would call 'asserting my identity,' so I can* *grow up to be a well-adjusted individual. Sure, I say I want freedom, but without parental supervision I'm much more likely to smoke pot and stuff. I hope my parents don't try to act like my friends. What I really need are parents.*

What a difference between what kids say they want and what they know deep down they need. Parents who never discipline a child really don't care enough about him to go to the trouble—and perceptive kids understand that. We, too, have to be smart enough to grasp this same truth when it comes to our Father in heaven.

Ann Landers was famous for saying, "You should be happy you have a parent who punishes you, because it shows that your parent cares." Solomon, in the book of Proverbs,[45] says, "A parent who does not punish his child hates his child."

And we also get this message directly in the book of Deuteronomy.[46] "You should know in your heart that just as a father will chastise his son, so the Lord, your God, chastises you."

True, we shouldn't try to apply this principle in cases where the suffering is too severe. It isn't meant to explain why your Aunt Martha got terminal cancer. But it is one possible explanation for suffering, and it surely has relevance in many situations.

A young woman I know arrived at this conclusion herself after an experience where she had to administer medical treatment to her pet cat. As she tells it: "The cat had gotten an abscess in his cheek, which had to be drained by a vet.

Then to prevent the infection from spreading, the vet told me to reopen the wound once a day for several days and to flush out with an antibiotic solution any pus that might have built up. The procedure was very painful to the cat. Naturally, he struggled in my arms to escape the treatment. I felt so bad because this poor creature couldn't possibly understand how antibiotics work and that this was good for him, that this was preventing a far greater calamity. And it suddenly hit me that that's the way it is between God and us. We can't understand God's 'medicine,' which might be painfully administered, any more than this cat. We are just as ignorant, and even if it were explained to us we wouldn't get it. The only thing we can do is trust in God that it is good for us."

FROM THE BITTER COMES THE SWEET

There are several variations on the rebuke principle, all of which teach in different ways that suffering is sent by God not as punishment, but as a lesson. If we pay attention, we will find out in the long run that there was much good in the pain. The first illustration I want to give you might be called "from the bitter comes the sweet," and it is derived from a Biblical story about the bitter waters of Marah.[47]

Shortly after the Israelites escaped from bondage in Egypt and crossed the Red Sea, they came upon a spring at a place called Marah, which in Hebrew means "bitter." Having traveled three days through the desert without water, they were understandably very thirsty, but could not drink from this spring because the water was—you guessed it—bitter.

Of course, they got upset. Here they thought that God was on their side and from now on life would be an easy street—seas splitting whenever difficulties come up—but suddenly comes this challenge. What could this bitter place be doing in the middle of the smooth path of life?

Obviously, God had placed this trial in their way to teach them—and teach us, reading it thousands of years later—a very important lesson. So let's examine carefully exactly what the Biblical story means.

Here is what happened next: In response to the anguished complaints of the Israelites, God told Moses to take a branch from a nearby tree that in itself was bitter. In effect, God said, here is the cure: "Take the bitter tree and throw it into the bitter water." And lo and behold, the waters became sweet.

What were the Jews taught at Marah? First, the reality of life that just because you're a believer doesn't mean you'll never experience difficulties. Life isn't meant, as the cliché goes, to be a bowl of cherries. And this was a particularly appropriate lesson immediately after the incredible miracle of the Red Sea splitting. Just because they were the beneficiaries of a supernatural blessing doesn't mean that from then on their lives would always have fairy-tale endings. Problems are the rent we pay for the right to live on Earth.

But there is a more important message that God gave us at the place of the bitter waters. There is a secret for transforming life's bitterness. There is a way to turn bitter waters to sweet. Amazingly enough, it is to *use the bitter itself in order to bring about turning bad to good!*

Impossible, you say? At the very close of the Marah story, the Bible adds, incongruously, "For I am the Lord, your healer [doctor]." Now consider the remarkable coincidence that this very principle of "from bitter comes the sweet" became, centuries later, the basis of a breakthrough in man's understanding of medicine and the healing process.

Without a doubt, one of the greatest achievements of medical science has been the invention of vaccines. Naturally, back in 1796, doctors were appalled when Edward Jenner first proposed injecting a healthy man with a small amount of cowpox culture in order to render him immune to smallpox. Introduce the very disease we're trying to eliminate into the body of a healthy patient? The idea seemed preposterous. Use the bitter to make it better? Who ever heard of such an absurdity? Jenner's critics scoffed. But of course that very proposal had already been broached before. It came from none other than God Himself. Bitter introduced into the water made the water sweet. Smallpox introduced into the body produced the powerful antibodies that would ultimately conquer the sickness. The concept of vaccination worked, and a whole new field of medicine was born. And that must be why God, at the conclusion of the Marah story, refers to Himself as a doctor. After all, He had just demonstrated what it would take medical genius several thousand years more to discover.

Today we understand that the injection of the vaccine—

"the bitter"—into a person triggers a response in the immune system, causing it to strengthen itself. Then, when an epidemic hits, the immune system has the means to fight back and overcome the disease. From the bitter comes sweet. What the rabbis took from this story, though, was even more than a medical breakthrough. This very same principle—from the bitter comes the sweet—finds application in all of life. The bitterness we often experience, the pains and suffering of our daily existence, may very well be the "vaccines" that protect us from far more serious complications. Problems build up our spiritual immune systems. Difficulties overcome make us far stronger. We grow not from our sweet moments, but from our setbacks.

There is a story told of a meeting between the famed twentieth-century sage known as the Chofetz Chayim and a former student.

"How is everything?" asked the rabbi.

"Bad," replied the student.

"Don't say it's 'bad,'" admonished Chofetz Chayim, "say it's 'bitter.'"

The student was perplexed, not understanding the difference. "But, Rabbi, either way, I am saying the same thing."

"No, my son, not at all," the great rabbi replied. "Bad is far from the same as bitter. A medicine may be bitter, but it is never bad!"

Bitter is a temporary taste sensation. Castor oil is bitter. Medicine is bitter, but we don't say it's bad because we recognize that something can be bitter for the moment, but have long-range beneficial effects.

The bitter taste of God's medicine, sufferings we may have to endure today, can very well have the effect of our healing tomorrow.

THE STRUGGLE FOR STRENGTH

Another variation on the rebuke principle takes this idea of using pain to build strength even further. To illustrate, I will use two more examples from nature.

The first comes from the life of John Audubon, the great naturalist and ornithologist. One day, he observed a beautiful butterfly fluttering in distress, unable to detach itself from its cocoon. Touched by the creature's pain, he gently set it free by cutting open the cocoon. It flew a few feet and then dropped dead. As he later learned, nature had fastened it to the cocoon, where it was forced to flutter until the muscles of its wings were strong enough to fly. By setting it free too soon, by "making it easier for the poor butterfly," he had doomed it to death.

Nature teaches us a powerful lesson: Painful experiences strengthen us for the greater challenges in life that are destined to follow.

The other story from nature involves another kind of creature that develops in a cocoon—a moth. Leroy B. Grant pointed out that, like the butterfly, the moth too must struggle to emerge from its cocoon, but through that struggle it drives various cocoon poisons from its body. Without the struggle, it would die.

Grant concluded, "When people struggle for what they want, they become stronger and better, but if things come too easily, they become weak and something in them seems to die."

We all have seen children grow into caring, self-reliant adults because they had to struggle for everything they earned. Those who weren't born with a silver spoon in their mouth were driven to achieve what children of privilege never could accomplish. Kirk Douglas has been quoted as saying, "My children never had my advantage of being born in abject poverty." Adversity makes us stronger, and it has a teaching dimension. It hones us and makes us better human beings.

A poem by Robert Browning Hamilton gets the point across beautifully:

I walked a mile with Pleasure, she chattered all the way,
But never a thing do I recall of what she had to say.
I walked a mile with Sorrow and never a word said she,
But oh, the things I learned from her when Sorrow spoke to me.

CHAPTER 11

THE TEST OF ABRAHAM

We began this book with a discussion about the book of Job. We considered whether the equation could logically exist that God is good and just and all-powerful while, at the same time, bad things happen to good people. We've tried to show how it's possible to answer that question in the affirmative.

But this discussion would not be complete without examining another famous Biblical story that raises similar questions in its own right—the story of Abraham and God's demand that he sacrifice his son Isaac.

This is a story of a man who—in a world filled with idolatry and polytheism—comes to the conclusion that there is only One God. With that he is the father of monotheism as we know it today. He is a wonderful man—the epitome of loving-kindness.

Yet God inflicts upon him a terrible choice: Sacrifice your son or disobey your God.

We look at his story now and say, "Well, it all turned out well in the end." But can you imagine being Abraham and having no way of knowing what the final outcome would be? Can you picture him at the top of the mountain feeling that obedience to God means he has to be ready to kill the very son that God had promised him late in life as the father of future generations?

Abraham suffered. There can be no question about it.

Add to that the fact that Abraham, the believer, had two brothers, both of whom had many children. He had none. He had grown to be an old man, and he had no heirs. Finally, when he was one hundred and his wife was ninety, God promised him a child—a son—and delivered on that promise. But just when he finally had a chance to enjoy this boy and to plan for his future, God appeared to him with this bizarre request.

We call it a test. But who needs tests like this? Why did he have to be tested? What is this all about?

Was God trying to see what Abraham would do? Surely God, who is all-knowing, had a fairly good idea of the outcome, so why put Abraham through this horror?

Some of the finest Jewish philosophers and theologians, among them the greats Maimonides (Rabbi Moses Ben Maimon, 1135–1204) and Nachmanides (Rabbi Moses Ben Nachman, 1194–1270), have pondered this story. They were the two masters of Biblical interpretation in the Middle Ages, and each one approached the problem from a different angle. Now which one is correct—Maimonides or Nachmanides? I believe that the real answer is a combination of both.

It is interesting to note that when modern scholars analyzed what they said and compared their opinions with older texts of the Midrash, they found that both the views of Maimonides and Nachmanides had already been offered—not in philosophical terms, but in Midrashic language that favors stories and parables.

The ways in which Nachmanides and Maimonides explain Abraham's test, a test accompanied by incalculable pain, provide two more concepts with which we can make sense of our own moments of suffering. I call these the "actualization principle" (as explained by Nachmanides) and the "education principle" (as explained by Maimonides).

THE ACTUALIZATION PRINCIPLE

Nachmanides argues that man has freedom of choice. It is up to him to either do something or to refrain from doing it. God knows what man's decision will be when confronted with a difficult choice. But that doesn't mean that we can avoid going through the decision process. God's knowledge doesn't *create* reality; it only *foretells* it. For man to achieve spiritual greatness, it isn't enough for God to know that he could theoretically pass a test. Until a demonstration of faith is actually performed, it remains no more than potential. God doesn't judge us by what we *might* become; He allows us the opportunity to *actualize* our character traits and to demonstrate ultimate commitment. Then God can reward us not for our intentions, but for our deeds. That's why God very often gives us tests, just as teachers do to their students. A good teacher will be able to predict how her students will fare with a great degree of precision. She knows which ones will apply themselves, study the material and do well, and which ones won't. So why does she give the tests anyway? She gives the tests in order for the students to be motivated to study and attain a greater level of knowledge, to bring to fruition all that they are capable of becoming.

Abraham had tremendous spiritual strength. There was no doubt that he was capable of tremendous self-sacrifice. God knew Abraham's greatness. By presenting Abraham with the test, God allowed him to convincingly prove it.

The sacrifice of Isaac—which more accurately is called the "binding" of Isaac, since there never was any sacrifice—was the last of ten trials that God put Abraham through. This story is the most famous because it is the toughest and the last of these ten tests.

In Hebrew, the word *nes,* which means test, interestingly enough also has three other meanings: *Nes* means to be uplifted or elevated; *nes* means a flag or a banner that is held up high; *nes* also means miracle.

How are all these related? What makes them share the same word? A test is the same as a banner held up high; in passing his test, Abraham was *elevated.* Abraham became what a flag or banner represents: a symbol of greatness that can inspire others. And when a person passes such a test and is so elevated, that is indeed a miracle—the miracle of human beings rising to the level of their potential. How wondrous to see that we are able to accomplish what no one would ever dream is in the realm of the possible!

I know of a woman who believed herself to be close to God. She frequently participated in various mind-expanding New Age workshops and was fond of expounding on the meaning of spirituality. One day, as she was deep in prayer, she said, "God, you know I would do anything for you. Just do not test me through my children."

A few days later, she learned that her adult son had been diagnosed with leukemia. He eventually died, and she was sent into a terrible tailspin, reexamining herself, her faith and her relationship to God. She emerged from a horrendous period of grief, stronger, more authentically religious and, as she herself maintains, a better person.

Of course, she should not have dared God. But once she opened the door to a reality she never believed she could overcome, it somehow became necessary for the test to actually take place.

Such experiences, in their very harshness, allow us to actualize strengths that otherwise are known not even to ourselves, but only to God.

The famed Danish philosopher Søren Kierkegaard argued that Abraham was not asked to sacrifice his son as much as he was asked to sacrifice his intelligence, since the whole notion of sacrificing his son didn't make sense. Previously, God had told Abraham, "You will have a future through your son. Your descendants will be more numerous than the stars." And then God says to kill him. The test was whether Abraham could obey a command from God even though it was irrational, even though it went counter to everything God had told him before. It was his total faith in this God that was being tested.

He had to demonstrate that he was willing to carry out this illogical act because he believed in God. *Abraham could not have been what he was unless he consented.*

To say that God knew in advance that Abraham would pass the test proves nothing. Yes, God knew that once Abraham faced the challenge of fulfilling his potential, he would. But it would be false to say that God knew the outcome in advance, and because of that He didn't have to put Abraham through the test. Unless Abraham actually passed the test, he couldn't become his best self.

It was the test that allowed Abraham the opportunity to actualize the meaning of faith and the concept of sacrificing all for one's beliefs. He demonstrated the idea that there are times when we must follow God even when it is illogical. I can just picture God saying to Himself, "I know he is going to pass the test, so that is why I am giving it to him. I am giving him the test precisely because I know he is going to pass."

So Nachmanides concludes that until Abraham actually experienced his trials and lived through them, his capacity for faith and loyalty was only potential. His qualities were not yet forged into the very essence of his character.

THE METAPHOR OF THE VESSELS

Making the same point, the Midrash[48] offers the following analogy about a potter.

> *To test a vessel for his kiln, a potter taps it at various spots to see if it gives forth a characteristic ring, indicating that it is free from cracks or other defects. But if a vessel is obviously broken or even shows a definite crack, there is no need to test it. It is clearly defective.*
>
> *By analogy then, if heaven subjects someone to a test, it indicates that a person has already achieved much. He appears to be whole, morally strong. Wicked people, however, are never tested as Abraham and Job were. With their moral defect or weakness, any trial would only bring another moral downfall. For this, heaven has no wish.*
>
> *The message seems to be very clear. The potter has to check out his merchandise. But if the merchandise is obviously defective, there is no need for a test because the outcome is known—the vessel will break. A vessel that may be strong or may have hidden flaws is one that should be tested. If it does not break, it can then be guaranteed as a worthy vessel.*

The Midrash is telling us that good people are more likely to endure the travails of God's trials than the wicked because for the wicked the outcome of the test is a foregone conclusion. For them a test is pointless. The upright, how-ever, are given the choice to rise to the occasion and achieve their potential.

I am reminded of Helen Keller, a remarkable woman who has inspired millions of people. God knew that Helen Keller could handle the challenge presented to her. Because of her handicaps, which she overcome with such aplomb, Helen Keller became a greater person than she would have been had she been born on easy street.

She was given many tests in her life as she learned to speak, then went on to Radcliffe, graduated with honors, and became a famous writer and lecturer. Her trials were steppingstones to a higher level of being. And she found the wisdom to write, "Character cannot be developed in ease and quiet. Only through experience of trial and suffering can the soul be strengthened, ambition inspired and success achieved."

Surely as a result of her afflictions, her soul became ele-vated. Passing her many tests, she could look back at her life and conclude, "Many persons have a wrong idea of what constitutes true happiness. It is not attained through self-gratification, but through fidelity to a worthy purpose."

Life offers us the opportunity to see many other similar examples. It is no longer uncommon to see a handicapped person competing in a challenging sport—people missing legs running in marathons or skiing, people in wheelchairs playing basketball, deaf people performing as actors. Let me share with you one moving illustration:

Once a year there's a twenty-six-mile marathon in New York City. Many tens of thousands of people participate. Crowds come to cheer for the winner. I want to tell you the story of the "loser"—the person who came in dead last in 1998, many hours after everyone had already completed the race.

Her name is Zoe Koplowitz. She was forty-six years old, and she suffered from a debilitating disease—multiple sclerosis. She'd had it more than twenty years. She walked on two crutches, one slow painful step at a time. She walked for twenty-seven hours and thirty-four minutes and finished the marathon. She came in last, but she finished. She limped across the finish line with her left leg dragging.

Why did she do it? Here was her answer:

> *When you are born, God gives you a television set with a hundred channels. Ninety-nine of them have wonderful programs on them. One has only static. Everybody, with no exceptions, has that channel with the static on their set. The only difference is the kind of static you were given on that one channel. And you have a choice. You can sit in front of that one channel for the rest of your life and look at the static, or you can get up and change the channel. My commitment in life is to change the channel as frequently as possible.*

We *can* rise above our physical and emotional handicaps. We *can* change the channel as so many of those so challenged have shown us. And they typically testify that as a result of the experiences that have so tested them, they are stronger and better human beings.

THE EDUCATION PRINCIPLE

Now let's give another major Jewish philosopher and theologian a hearing on the reason for the test of Abraham. Maimonides reads the story of the trial of the sacrifice of Isaac a little differently. Not that he disagrees totally with the analysis of Nachmanides. It is just that he gives the story—and its point—another emphasis.

Maimonides sees the purpose of the test as education for the rest of mankind. God tested Abraham—knowing that the patriarch would measure up to the test—to demonstrate to the rest of the world the possibilities of human perfection, the spiritual heights flesh and blood could achieve.

It's as if the potter were testing his vessel in the store in order to impress and convince others of the high quality of his merchandise.

This revelation by God—using Abraham as the vessel—was meant not only for his contemporaries, but for the benefit of all future generations. God knew that millions of people would one day read this story in the Bible and be inspired.

God wanted Abraham to pass this tremendously difficult trial so that his story could stand as proof of the power of faith. And who knows if that didn't help countless of Abraham's descendants survive their own tests of faith when, during Crusades, pogroms or the Holocaust, Jews were confronted with the slaughter of their own children.

Examples of incredible obedience to God are what make it possible for people to follow in their ways.

So Maimonides is saying, in effect, that God needed inspirational characters for His storybook. God needed the originals to do those great things—overcoming all odds—so that we could learn from them.

Of course, Abraham could not have known that or even suspected it, or the test would have been a sham. In this very same way, someone today might be put through a divine trial without ever realizing the tremendous impact its successful resolution will have on others!

For example, a woman who has unexpectedly lost her husband and is deep in grief for the lost potential of their marriage cannot see how her sorrow might be of benefit to anyone else. Later on, perhaps when people tell her, "You were such an inspiration to me—the way you handled the death of your husband with such dignity . . . ," she can come to see that her loss was, in some ways, a spiritual gain, not just to herself but also to many others. That is what's meant by "being used in the service of God."

According to Maimonides, God wants to show us what his special people are made of. It's as if God is saying, "I've got some pots that are so strong you can hardly believe it with your own eyes. Watch, I am going to hammer that pot, and it still won't break. You have to appreciate the outstanding quality of these extraordinary vessels."

Why are you taught this demonstration? So that you, too, can be such a vessel. Pay careful attention and see what human beings are capable of. Faith can make a clay pot as strong as iron.

In this vein, I can't help but think of my father, of blessed memory. He had been through many trials and tribulations in his life, but I never heard him complain. He had to flee Nazi-occupied Europe. He had to learn another language late in life and start all over in America.

Life for his generation of immigrants was not easy, but he overcame all his difficulties. He made sacrifices, suffered, yet never lost his faith in God. I would often wonder if I would have been able to endure what he did.

To this day, one of my most vivid memories of my father is visiting him during the time of his last illness. He asked me to bend over close so that he might whisper something to me. He knew that he would soon be leaving this Earth, and this is what he chose to impress upon me: "My beloved Benny, I must tell you I do not understand why God found me worthy to bless me with so much throughout the days of my life."

I still cannot fathom the depth of piety that allowed him to reflect on his past—a past filled with so very much pain—and perceive it only from the perspective of the great goodness of the Almighty. Did he forget all the suffering? Did his mind play tricks upon him at the end? I don't think so. Not at all. It was his saintly nature that always emphasized the good over the bad and that to this day I try so hard to emulate.

The story of the test of Abraham could be rewritten with a somewhat different story line and substituting other names for the characters—the name of my father, my name, your name, every one of us who has been put through a test in life. And truth be told, who hasn't?

God gives us tests all the time, and if we understand that correctly, it's actually a heavenly compliment: It means that God feels we can handle them. The people who fail are a lot like intelligent students taking the finals. Some get 100 percent. Others get 75 percent, but they clearly had the potential to get 100 percent. Still others—with the same potential—flunk the test.

Why? It was their choice. They exercised their free will to flunk the test. But it doesn't mean that they should have flunked it. God knew that they should have passed it; they decided not to. And more often than not, they are angry with God for their own failings.

There is a better way, if we learn to think of the various moments in our own lives when we must face the challenges of adversity as our personal tests—tests that serve as divine instruments to encourage our spiritual growth as well as great opportunities to become heroic role models for those nearest and dearest to us.

CHAPTER 12

THE BALANCING FACTOR

O ne of the great kings of the Israelites was Hezekiah, a holy man who taught the Lord's ways to the nation. But somehow his teachings escaped his own son, Manasseh, who succeeded his father as king at age twelve and, not long after, became an idol worshiper. All the labors his father lavished upon him as a child did not bring him to the right path.

But then something changed Manasseh.

In the midst of a battle, his Assyrian enemies captured him. And this turn of events brought about an incredible transformation.

Plain and simple, it was suffering that caused Manasseh to turn to God. Why? Because in his new circumstance there was simply nobody else to turn to. And then, when the haughty young man was on his knees, humbled before God at last, the Almighty heard his prayers and brought him back to his kingdom in Jerusalem, where he again worshiped the one God.

This story brings us to another answer for why people suffer. I call it the "humility principle."

THE HUMILITY PRINCIPLE

The concept of a need for humility as a reason for suffering is introduced in the Talmud[49] in a very interesting way.

As the tale begins, the great Rabbi Eliezer is ill, suffering terribly. Visitors come to console him on his sickbed and among them are four sages of the day: Rabbi Tarfon, Rabbi Joshua, Rabbi Elazar Ben Azaria and Rabbi Akiva.

Rabbi Tarfon tells him, "You are more precious than the rain, because rain is only for this world, and you, Rabbi Eliezer, are for this world and the next."

With this poetic phrase, he seems to be telling Rabbi Eliezer, in effect, "Don't worry. God can't possibly take you away because the people who need your teaching, like a parched earth needs the rain, can't do without you. Therefore, God is not going to let you die any more than God is going to halt the rain, which is essential to life." Or he could also be saying to Rabbi Eliezer, "Don't worry because your teachings will live beyond you, because you have been like the rain that subsequently will cause fruit to grow."

Then Rabbi Joshua speaks up, "You are more valuable to Israel than the sun. The sun is but for this world, while you are for this world and the next."

Rabbi Joshua seems to have found another poetic phrase to echo the words of Rabbi Tarfon.

Then Rabbi Elazar Ben Azaria speaks, "You are to us more important than a father and a mother. Parents are for this world. They bring a child into this world, but you are for this world and the next."

Again, a similar poetic phrasing, although this comparison is more personal than the previous.

Rabbi Tarfon, Rabbi Joshua and Rabbi Elazar Ben Azaria, while consoling their friend, seem also to be verbalizing to God how important he is to them. They are saying, "Look God, look how we feel. Look how we need this man."

But then comes the final statement from the master, Rabbi Akiva. He says simply, "Suffering is precious."

The others emphasized to Rabbi Eliezer that his suffering would have to end soon because he meant too much to them. They were, in effect, negating what was happening.

Rabbi Akiva, on the other hand, not only accepted what was happening, but he elevated it. He found a positive aspect to it. Suffering is valuable, precious.

At this, Rabbi Eliezer perks up. He asks to sit up so he can listen better. And he demands, "Akiva, how do you know this? Where in the Bible do you find such a statement?"

And Rabbi Akiva[50] cites the story of Manasseh as his source. He concludes that from this narrative we learn how precious suffering can be. Suffering is an educational experience. It enters the picture when one hasn't learned a lesson because things are going too well. When one is on top of the world and not open to hearing God, suffering brings the message of humility, precisely because it is such a humbling experience.

Now the Talmud does not suggest, nor am I suggesting, that Rabbi Eliezer needed to learn humility. All he needed to hear was that there is a message in suffering and that he should ask God what it is. Rabbi Akiva was merely introducing a concept:

- Suffering has a purpose.
- When Manasseh suffered, he learned a lesson he needed to learn, which for him was humility.
- The lesson in suffering is what makes it precious.
- Rabbi Eliezer had an obligation to introspect and discover what God was trying to say to him through his suffering.

We are all familiar with people like Manasseh, people with wise parents, but who never acquire wisdom on their own. They are kids who have everything—and therefore they appreciate nothing.

I know a young man who grew up with a father who was an extremely successful, self-made man. The father worked long hours from his youth and built a multimillion-dollar business. He didn't want his son to undergo the same deprivations he endured. Remembering how he walked and took the bus everywhere, the father gave his son, for the son's sixteenth birthday, a car—and not just any car, but a top-of-the-line Jaguar. What followed soon afterwards is unfortunately all too common: cutting school for joy rides, showing off to his peers by driving them everywhere (which left little time for homework), boredom with classes that couldn't compare to the excitement of his "credit-card excursions." It didn't take long for the son to get into trouble with the law. It was the story of Manasseh repeating itself. It's not easy to become a king at age twelve, with the world at your fingertips and no one daring to contradict you. How do you learn humility?

Manasseh learned it in captivity, and so did this young man. Not until he was arrested and spent a few days in jail did he get shaken up. He realized there were situations from which even his father's money couldn't save him. It took a little suffering early in life to learn a lesson for which this young man will someday be tremendously grateful.

There are many more modern-day illustrations that come to mind. There are people who are sitting on top of the world, who have forgotten everything—their friends, where they came from, that God runs the world. They forget that they, too, are human. We see people like that, and sometimes we wish that something would happen that would put them in their place a little bit.

So suffering—as this answer, which is just one of many approaches we want to keep in mind—accomplishes that. It serves as a teaching experience on the part of God to bring a person back to a reality with which they lost touch when things were going too well.

In the Bible we have the recurring story of Amalek and his

people, the quintessential evil nation of anti-Semites, whose existence seems always to remind the Israelites who they are and who God is. Amalek pops up on the scene whenever the Israelites stray from their covenant with God, forget what their mission in this world is supposed to be and begin squabbling with one another.

The Bible teaches that Amalek—and the suffering he inflicted—existed in order to help God solve a problem. Whenever Amalek attacked, the Jews remembered God, and they united to fight a common enemy. The Talmud[51] says that forty-eight prophets and seven prophetesses—warning the nation to repent and pray to God—couldn't accomplish what one Haman (a descendant of Amalek who plotted to kill all the Jews) was able to achieve overnight. All these prophets were standing there devoting their lives to preaching doom: "Please, Jews, listen and be good, be good, be good!" All to no avail. But once Haman presented the threat of extermination, the Jewish people suddenly, with uncharacteristic fervor, found themselves deep in prayer.

C. S. Lewis said, "Pain is God's megaphone to wake up a deaf world." When we have sufficient faith to believe that God is speaking to us through our pain, we will be wise enough to comprehend the message, and our suffering, now imbued with meaning, will be that much easier to bear.

THE ATONEMENT PRINCIPLE

Let's move on now to yet another fascinating idea offered by the sages. To understand this principle, we will examine another story from the Talmud.[52]

Rabbi Abohu is taking care of his father, who is suffering the ravages of old age, possibly the aftermath of a stroke. Rabbi Abohu's father asks him for a glass of water, which, as a dutiful son, he promptly goes to get. But when he returns with the water, his father has fallen asleep. Now, bent over his father, he is uncertain what to do. His father might wake up any second and want the water. He wouldn't want him to have to ask for it again. As he is standing there, not sure if he should continue to wait or leave, his mind suddenly focuses on a passage in the book of Psalms. He reflects on its meaning and finds himself discovering a new insight into its words. Never had he understood the real idea of Psalm 79 until this moment, because now he saw the connection between his father's suffering and a puzzling part of the passage.

Psalm 79 begins: "Oh God, the nations have . . . defiled Your holy sanctuary; they have made Jerusalem into heaps of ruins."

It is an extremely sad psalm by Asaph, describing the destruction of the temple. Unlike many of the psalms that are inspirational in nature and are called "songs of ascent," this psalm is mournful. Yet if you pick up any book of Psalms, you will find it headed "A *song* of Asaph." This is what was bothering Rabbi Abohu. Why a song? A song is by nature happy, uplifting. This is a poem about tragedy; why was it not called a lamentation?

And then it came to him that the composer, Asaph, saw something positive about the destruction of the temple, long regarded as the greatest tragedy that befell the Jewish people. How could that be? Well, reasoned Rabbi Abohu, because God was angry at the transgressions of His people, He opted to destroy a building of stone and wood when He could have just as easily have destroyed the Israelite nation instead. This was something that had given Asaph so much solace that he named his composition a song and not a lamentation.

As this insight flashed through his mind, Rabbi Abohu related this to a passage from the book of Lamentations,[53] which speaks of the sorrow of the Jewish people at the destruction of the temple. "The Lord has spent His fury; He has poured out His fierce anger; and He has kindled a fire in Zion that has consumed His foundation."

This also suggests that a good thing had happened. There is a positive aspect in the destruction of the temple. True, the enemies of the Israelites came and destroyed their holiest shrine, the symbol of their unique relationship with God. But it could have been worse. "The Lord has *spent* His fury." By allowing this to happen, God considered the need for anger to be over. Payment for sin has been exacted, and justice is now considered served. The Jewish people may live.

Now let's not forget that Rabbi Abohu is having these

insights as he is standing with a glass of water bent over his elderly father. He is watching the ravages of a stroke on his father's face; he is studying the way suffering has undermined a once vibrant human being.

He is thinking, *Why did this happen? How could this be?* And then he realized that perhaps this, too, is a kind of atonement. Maybe, just like when a temple of stone and wood was razed, so too a temporal body of blood and flesh was afflicted. But the human being is still alive. He has been spared. It could have been worse.

There is a well-known Yiddish saying, *Oy, zol zein a kapparah!* (Let it be an atonement!) Maybe something worse was deserved, but thankfully that more terrible thing didn't happen.

In the old days, this expression was used when people survived a dreadful experience. A person had a heart attack. A person suffered a severe financial reversal. It was said: "Let it be an atonement." Let it be that he paid his dues and now can start fresh again.

I have seen people go through cycles like this. Everything goes wrong, and it seems they are living in a disaster zone. And then suddenly everything turns around, and things start to go right again. And one wonders: Maybe this was an atonement, which is now complete.

I know a man whose child was critically ill. The prognosis was grave. Then, as if to add to his grief, the stock market crashed (this was in 1987), and he lost a fortune. Yet, almost immediately thereafter his child got well to the utter amazement of the doctors. His financial loss was an obvious atonement, a *kapparah,* for what could have been a far greater loss.

That is the essence of the atonement principle. Since you have to pay your dues one way or another, then perhaps some of the ways you do that—and which may appear very bad on the surface—can be viewed as serving the purpose of compensation for wrongs committed.

So a person loses his job or becomes ill—only God knows why—but it could balance out a wrong. We often lose sight of what we still have when we suffer a loss or experience a seemingly terrible "act of God." And perhaps the reason why we're still permitted, by the heavenly scales of justice, to retain our blessings is that we have paid for them by the coin of suffering.

CHAPTER 13

NOT OF THIS WORLD

O f course, there is still more. None of the individual explanations are meant to solve all of our Job-like moments. Yet every one of them applies at some point and for some people.

The answers we are about to consider in this chapter have one interesting thing in common. Basic to their understanding is a belief in—or at least a recognition of—another dimension, a spiritual world that exists unseen by us, but which parallels the world we know—the so-called *olam haba,* the next world or the world-to-come.

I call the first of the answers in this category the "tradeoff principle." This principle states that you are better off getting punished for your transgressions in this world and rewarded for your good deeds in the next world.

The Talmud[54] illustrates this idea by recounting a remarkable incident.

Again, our friend Rabbi Eliezer is sick, but this time it is his students who come to visit. He says to them, "There is a fierce wrath in the world." And they break down in tears. But just then the legendary Rabbi Akiva comes in and starts to laugh.

"Why do you laugh?" they inquire of him.

"Why do you weep?" he retorts, in the typically Jewish way of answering a question with a question.

"This holy man is dying. Should we not weep?"

"For that very reason, I rejoice. I had thought that he had received all his reward in this world, leaving nothing for the next. But now that I see him lying in pain, I rejoice knowing that his reward has been stored up for him in the next."

Then Rabbi Eliezer asks, "Akiva, I don't understand why this is happening to me. What could I have done wrong?"

And Rabbi Akiva answers, "You yourself taught us, for there is not a just man upon Earth who does only good and sins not."

This story is pregnant with meaning. Rabbi Eliezer is suffering from illness. He is trying to understand why it is happening to him, and the only thing he comes up with as an explanation is that there is a fierce anger in the world. It must be, he seems to be saying, that the rest of the world deserves God's punishment, and I am simply caught up in the storm of divine wrath.

But Rabbi Akiva points out that that could not be true. You, Rabbi Eliezer, can't be completely good, just as the rest of the world can't be completely bad. The reality of the world is far more profound.

I have to agree. I have seen all kinds of weird mixtures within people. I have seen despicable human beings, and yet to be honest, I have to say that even they had virtues. One individual I know is a terror in business. His employees cower before him, shed tears and complain that he is giving them ulcers. But at home, he is a patient and devoted husband and father. Home and office are literally different worlds to him. At home he is a saint, at work a monster.

We have in Deuteronomy confirmation of this view that no one is all good or all bad:[55] "But He [God] pays back his enemies to their face in order to destroy them. He does not delay the payment that He gives His enemies to their face." Even God's enemies deserve payment. No, not punishment, but *payment*—the Biblical word for *reward*! Why? Because it is simply inconceivable that even those we call evil don't have at least some redeeming virtues, some moments in which they performed acts of kindness. They, too, have to be *paid back* for their good deeds. The only thing that God chooses to do differently with them is to alter the time frame for reward and punishment.

Whatever reward an evil man is supposed to get for being occasionally good, he will get "to his face," that is, during his lifetime, in this world. The fact that the wicked prosper, according to this analysis, is not a problem, but is rather a solution. It is a way to get the bad people compensated for their good behavior here, rather than in the next world, where they will receive only punishment.

On the other hand, for good people, the system operates in precisely the opposite order. For whatever sins they may have committed—and "there is no one so righteous upon this Earth who does only good"—they suffer here on Earth. That is what their souls prefer so that they can come to the other world with a totally clean slate. Far better the rewards of heaven than its punishment; far better the pain of Earth than its foolish delights.

That is why Rabbi Akiva says, in effect, "I used to worry about you, my teacher. I saw everything was going well for you. Nothing bad ever happened to you. So I feared that all the bad would have to happen to you there. But now that I see you getting a measure of suffering, I say, thank God."

The tradeoff concept says that the wicked have it go well with them on Earth because they are using up their bank account here for whatever good they did do. Meanwhile, in another dimension, a debit account is being kept of their misdeeds, and in the place of eternal judgment they will have to settle up. The good people, on the other hand, suffer on Earth, because they are paying as they go and storing up the merits of their good deeds in the world-to-come.

In other words, if you don't get it here, you'll get it there.

The wicked get the reward here because they are going to get punished there. For the good it must be just the reverse. As a matter of fact, if the good seem to be getting overly rewarded here, then one might worry. That's exactly what Rabbi Akiva was thinking: *Oh my goodness, my teacher is living too well.* He was troubled because he understood this principle of tradeoff.

There are subtleties to this that further clarify the appropriate place for reward—whether God chooses to repay the performance of good deeds in the here and now or in the hereafter. For example, let's say we have a good person trying to fulfill the commandment of giving to charity, but he doesn't do it with an open heart. He isn't really sincere. He is only interested in the recognition that a charitable gift will bring him. He wants a large plaque on the door. God rewards such a false good deed—a deed lacking in truth—in a world that is lacking in truth, with payments that are lacking in truth. So, yes, the person gets his recognition, the plaque, the reward, the write-up in the paper. And that's all. Meanwhile, the person who gives with a pure heart, seeking nothing, is giving in truth. And that's why his reward will be in the world of truth, in the world-to-come.

Most important of all, God knows who is who. He looks into the soul of every human being, and He knows who will appreciate which kind of reward. God not only repays acts of goodness and punishes sinful deeds; He even picks the place for reward or punishment in accord with our own spiritual desires.

There is a law in the Bible[56] that you have to give a worker his wages immediately, right after he completes his task.

There is only one exception: if he doesn't want to be paid immediately because he understands that if he defers payment until later, his reward will be greater. So, too, God pays back in accord with the desire of His "workers." The understanding of people determines God's method of payment. The evil man would rather—because he only sees what is in front of him—have the reward here immediately, so God does that for him. The righteous man would prefer not to get it here, and so God accommodates him as well.

EXCEPTIONS TO THE TRADEOFF PRINCIPLE

But if things worked only this way, we would suspect anyone who was living comfortably of being an evil person! Therefore, Maimonides made it very clear that there are exceptions to the rule.

In the book of Deuteronomy[57] we find a passage that strongly suggests that reward for good people who obey God's commandments does indeed come on this Earth:

> *If you thoroughly heed My commandments that I am commanding you today—to love the Lord your God, and to serve Him with all your desires and with your entire beings, I will provide the rain in your land in its time, the fall rain and spring rain, and you will harvest your grain and your wine and your olive oil. And I will provide grass in your field for your animals, and you will eat and be full.*

Maimonides clarifies that in this passage God is not speaking of reward, but of sustenance. A good person, obeying God's commandments, will be sustained and supported in order to continue his good works because he is a partner with God in doing things that God wants. In other words, God will be *using* him, rather than *rewarding* him.

Let us take for an example a person who engages in the good work of feeding the world's hungry. That person is God's partner, so God takes care of him. It's as if God is saying to a good person, "Keep up the good work. I will send you the funds and whatever else you need because you are handling it well." When a person does a good job, God sends him things on a regular basis to preserve a mutually beneficial partnership.

This explains, according to Maimonides, why good people are sometimes successful and do have money. It is because God sees that they handle their wealth correctly. Their wealth is not so much their reward as it is placed in their care for safekeeping and for redistribution.

But Maimonides also gives us another reason to explain what we now (remarkably enough) consider a problem: the *success* of the righteous. He points out that the Ten Commandments were given on two stone tablets because they represent two categories of law. The first set contains laws governing the relationship between man and God; the second set summarizes laws governing the relationship between man and man. Interestingly enough, Maimonides asserts, God's system of reward and punishment differs accordingly.

The commandments that man carries out or violates in relationship to God relate to heaven, so to speak, and they are recompensed in the next world. The others that deal with our interactions with people are rewarded in this world *and* in the next world. The Talmud[58] states: "These are the things for which a man eats the fruits in this world but whose principal remains intact for him in the world-to-come. They are honoring father and mother, acts of kindness, early attendance at the house of study morning and evening, hospitality to guests, visiting the sick, providing for a bride, escorting the dead, absorption in prayer, bringing peace between man and his fellow."

The terminology here is very interesting—note the metaphor of fruit. Picture a fruit tree. Imagine a tree bearing apples. Its fruit is only a portion of the tree, but the tree is far more than the fruit. The apple tree, as a matter of fact, has the capacity to produce apples on a regular basis from year to year and to produce hundreds, thousands of them.

This world is but the *first* reward, just as the fruit is a product of a tree whose roots carry within them the power to produce so very much more. If you help people here, measure for measure, there must be some reward here as well. But that is but a minor expression of a far, far greater reward lying in wait—a root that will produce endlessly in the next world.

Now let's take an example from real life and apply this principle. Sarah is visiting the sick. She honors her parents. She gives charity. Her good deeds will be rewarded here—according to the measure-for-measure principle, which we had discussed in chapter 2—because she is improving this world. She will see the fruits of her goodness.

But Sarah is also God's partner in some of her good works. She is helping God to do those things that He desires to happen in this world. Because of this, God helps her to continue by granting her the health and the means to carry on. Of course, later, in the next world, she can expect a far more suitable and bountiful reward.

THE APPRECIATION PRINCIPLE

Let's move on now to the second principle in this chapter. It has its source in the story of the Garden of Eden. There, the first man and woman lived a life that was comfortable, easy, and . . . well . . . just paradise. But as children who have everything and therefore appreciate nothing, Adam and Eve didn't realize how good they had it. So, with their free will they made a conscious choice to disobey God, and they were forced to leave the Garden of Eden. Along with that exit came a rough way of life. "By the sweat of your brow you shall earn your bread,"[59] God told Adam. "In pain shall you give birth to your children,"[60] God told Eve.

Now the whole object of life on Earth became the quest to return to the place from which they were expelled. It's as if God had said, "Okay, the first time you had it easy, but you didn't appreciate it; now you will have to earn it."

Ideally, a human being should have everything readily accessible. Life should be so easy that whenever you feel like it, you could pluck a piece of fruit from the tree and eat. And you should be able to have children without any pain, and everything you want should come to you with a snap of the finger. It should be—but Adam and Eve made their choice, and we are stuck with it. But there is a positive side to the pain and suffering that comes with making it in life. With the hard work we put into acquiring what we need comes an appreciation and an understanding—indeed the knowledge of all things good and evil.

And to get that special knowledge, to get to that special place, we have to struggle.

Expounding on this idea, the Talmud[61] offers us this remarkable statement: "There are three things that can only be acquired through difficulty: understanding of Torah, the land of Israel and the world-to-come."

First, one has to labor to learn the lessons of the Bible. And this does not come to us handed on a silver platter. Even Moses had to do it. He got the Ten Commandments directly from God, but he broke them. And then he had to chisel out a second set all by himself. Every human being has to "chisel" out the meaning of life for himself; every person has to study the Bible in order to learn what God wants from him.

The second thing that can only be acquired with difficulty is the land of Israel. The Promised Land can't be realized simply by way of a promise. Human effort is required. Redemption isn't merely a gift; it must be fought for and earned. And the only way to achieve it is the hard way, through struggle. And why? Because only when you work for the land will you truly appreciate it.

The third in this series, *olam haba,* the world-to-come, can be understood in two ways. It can represent the next world, where we go when we die. It can also stand for the Messianic Era when there will be peace on Earth, and "the lion will lie down with the lamb."[62] Both the world-to-come and the coming world make demands upon us. They aren't unconditional divine promises. They are part of a covenant. Our part of the deal is to exert maximum effort; God's part of the promise is that our efforts will prove fruitful. But again, if God were to do it all for us, without any of "the sweat of our brows," we would never really appreciate it—just like we didn't have the good sense to appreciate paradise.

There is yet another story in the Talmud that teaches this concept.[63] At first glance it sounds like a fairy tale for children. It says that when you are in the womb, an angel lives with you there and teaches you everything you want to know about life—the entire Torah. But just when you are ready to be born the angel touches you on your upper lip—that's why you have a dimple there—and you forget everything you've learned.

Now what kind of a story is this?

Why would you be taught all the secrets of life, just so you would be made to forget them?

In its unique way, the Talmud makes the point that nothing is handed to you. For everything you must struggle. But it's not meant to be such a hard fight uphill after all. When you struggle to reach something, you don't have to learn it anew; you just have to remember it. But you have to struggle nonetheless so that you make it your own and appreciate what you have acquired. Like Moses of old, you have to carve out the tablets, so to speak, through your own effort. Then whatever you learn you will treasure as the work of your own hands, the product of your own labor.

I keep using simple illustrations, but they all make a point. The cooks who made something "from scratch" are so much prouder of their accomplishment than they would be if they made it from store-bought mix. Weekend gardeners are overjoyed as they point to their tomato crop and say, "I grew that tomato." For them, there are no tomatoes that could possibly taste as good anywhere else in the world. They needed God a little bit, too, but *it is their tomato*. What a feeling of accomplishment, simply because they put their sweat into it. Catch this phrase: They put their "sweat into it." It echoes the phrase from Genesis, "By the sweat of your brow you shall earn your bread."

In the Garden of Eden everything grew by itself. It was all, as the expression goes, "no sweat." But without sweat there could never be a gardener who could say, "I grew it myself. This is my tomato."

And that goes for anything that we acquire through hard work. You can't truly appreciate anything if you have not worked for it and acquired it through hardship. Only then can you say: This is mine. This is my insight. My land. My place in the next world.

So that's why all of human history, ever since Adam and Eve, took place outside of the Garden of Eden. It's only when we're not in a paradise that we can build one—and appreciate it when we finally get it.

CHAPTER 14

THE PUNISHMENT
OF MOSES

Moses, in the words of the Bible, was the greatest of all prophets, before or since. The Torah closes with a testimonial to his stature:

> *Never again arose in Israel a prophet like Moses, whom God had known face to face, as evidenced by all the signs and wonders that God sent him to perform in the land of Egypt, against Pharaoh and all his courtiers and all his land, and by all the strong hand and awesome power that Moses performed before the eyes of Israel.*[64]

And yet . . .

This same incredible individual was denied entry to the Promised Land. Moses had dedicated his whole life to this undertaking. He had endured forty years of hardship and strife in the wilderness while leading the stiff-necked Israelites, who were a constant source of stress and trouble for him. And then, just when he brought them to the very border as God commanded, he is told, "You do not deserve to fulfill your life's dream."

Moses pleads with God, but God only relents sufficiently to let him see the Promised Land from afar.

On the surface this seems a cruel and extreme punishment.

Why would God treat Moses so harshly? How could God deny the greatest leader of the Jewish people the right to complete his mission?

The answer of Jewish tradition is that, great as Moses was, he had still transgressed against God. He was told to speak to a rock from which water would flow. Instead, reacting in frustration at the constant griping of the Israelites, he struck the rock with his rod. By striking instead of speaking, he had not carried out God's command to the letter!

Can this really be ground for such severe punishment? After all, he hit a rock, not a human being. He didn't hurt anybody. Why such a big deal?

The answer of the rabbis is highly instructive: It might not have been a big deal in terms of the sin, but it was a big deal in terms of the sinner.

The French have a term for it. *Noblesse oblige,* literally "nobility obligates," means that honorable behavior above and beyond what is expected of commoners is an obligation of persons of high birth or rank.

Most of the world would probably say the opposite—the higher you go, the more you are above the law, can ignore the rules, get away with things. But according to the Bible, the higher you go, the *more* is expected of you for two reasons: You should know better, and you are supposed to be an example for everybody.

When someone like Moses loses his temper and strikes the rock, he is presenting a very poor role model. Imagine the impact on those witnessing this exhibition. Moses as leader is not entitled to the same kind of failings as we are. For him, the standard is not simply a passing grade; Moses must get a perfect mark.

More and better is expected of him, and so his actions are judged by a different standard.

This leads us to another concept through which we can better understand some cases of human suffering. I call it the "who-we-are principle."

It says simply: The suffering people endure in order to pay for their transgressions is meted out according to their station in life. The more worthy you are, the higher the spiritual level you aspire to, the more scrutiny you are under by God and the higher the standard by which your actions are judged.

There is an expression in Hebrew: *tzaddikim m'dakdek imohem k'chut ha'saroh,* which literally means "the righteous ones God deals with in strict measure as to a hairbreadth."

THE UNEXPLAINABLE

Now that we have covered a whole collection of insights as to why people suffer, we must examine yet one more

Talmudic statement that seems to set all that we have considered on its head. It is found in the *Ethics of the Fathers*.[65] Here we read the following statement in the name of Rabbi Yani: "It is not in our hands to grasp why the wicked are at ease or why the good suffer."

This, indeed, is a puzzling declaration. Is Rabbi Yani ignoring all the explanations found in the Talmud that deal with this very difficulty? Does he consider all those insights wrong? Is he saying there is no way you can solve the problem?

No.

But before I explain, let me tell you a little bit more about Rabbi Yani, so we can better understand his mind-set.

Here was a man who in his will specified that he should not be buried either in totally black garments, nor in totally white garments. He was obviously keeping in mind a tradition which teaches that at the time of the final redemption and resurrection of the dead, the dead will arise in the garments they were buried in—metaphorically, the good will rise in white garments and the wicked in black. Obviously, everyone wanted to be buried in white garments so as to rise up again among the good.

But Rabbi Yani wasn't about to pronounce himself totally righteous. He knew he wasn't perfect.

And for that very reason, he wasn't going to make such a judgment about others as well.

Talmudic commentators point out that Rabbi Yani's words have several meanings. His statement is more cryptic than it might at first appear. Why does he say, "It is not in our hands to grasp," when he could have said more clearly, "It is not in our power to understand"? Evidently, Rabbi Yani meant to specify that these puzzles are abstract—they are not things we can hold in our hands and turn over and examine at leisure. Further, why does he say, "The wicked are at ease," when he could have said, "The wicked prosper"? Again, he is not referring to the material, visible realities of life. He is talking about the intangibles of life—like being at ease, at peace. *That* is what he wanted to tell us is beyond our ability to comprehend.

Can we ever understand the lives of the Kennedys, who with all of their wealth weren't able to buy happiness? Can we come to grips with the lives of the Marilyn Monroes, who in spite of their fame couldn't buy peace of mind? Material prosperity, we've all too often learned, does not ensure contentment; capturing the headlines of the world doesn't bring with it automatic bliss. Yes, it is beyond our grasp to comprehend this. It is "not in our hands." Rabbi Yani added a powerful component to everything we've discussed until now. He asks us to look beyond the superficial ways in which we judge success—ways that make us question God's management of the world because, in our eyes, the wicked are "prospering" and the righteous "suffer." Include on the scale of judgment the psychological and mental response of people's reactions to their lot and you will come to a far different conclusion. Paupers may have peace of mind; princes may live out their lives in stress and anxiety. Ask who is really better off and the answer is exactly what Rabbi Yani emphasized: "It is not in our hands to grasp"!

ONLY FAITH HOLDS THE ANSWER

What Rabbi Yani may also be trying to teach us is that this question is of such a huge magnitude that it is not in our power *to fully explain* why the righteous suffer and why the wicked prosper.

At the end of the day, Rabbi Yani cautions us, this is a subject that we must approach with a certain amount of intellectual and spiritual humility. We won't be able to solve every puzzle. When Job could not fathom why these terrible things had happened to him, God finally told him, "It's beyond you to understand My ways."

If you have ever tried to explain a complex law of physics to a child, who lacks the intellect needed to grasp basic concepts, you can just imagine the bind God is in. He simply can't explain Einstein's Theory of Relativity to kindergarteners.

If we have so much trouble elucidating difficult ideas to children, how much greater is the impossibility of God clarifying complex concepts to us, with the gap between human and Divine comprehension approximating the size of infinity.

This, too, is included in Rabbi Yani's astute warning. "It is not in *our* hands." After all, we are still only human beings. Our judgments are fallible.

The bottom line, then, is that with all of our answers, we still need faith to permit us to maintain our belief.

Well, then, you will ask: "If that's so, why did we bother discussing all the other answers? What's the point of finding reasons when what we're left with is still faith? If we agree with Rabbi Yani that the enormity of the problem is beyond us, why didn't all the other rabbis throw in the towel and give up their search for meaning?"

The answer should be obvious:

There is a difference between blind faith and rational faith. Rabbi Yani didn't fundamentally disagree with all the other Talmudic scholars who preceded him. He wasn't trying to criticize all the rabbis who had offered brilliant insights into the theological puzzle of God's seeming unfairness. It would have been totally out of character for him to imply that everyone else was wrong and only his approach was right. And if that were indeed his intention, the Talmud would have followed his comment with the objections of all those who disagreed.

No, I am certain Rabbi Yani was supportive of every one of the ideas we have so diligently followed in the preceding chapters. To analyze, to probe and to seek ways to at least begin to understand the workings of God are to move from blind faith—a faith that can readily stumble because it lacks the light of any reason—to a rational faith that is rooted in the conclusion of an intellectual quest. Rational faith agrees that we don't have *all* of the answers; it takes heart from knowing that we didn't shy away from the questions. Rational faith makes its decision not simply in spite of the evil of this world; it affirms God because the reasons for belief in God based on

His goodness far outweigh the need to reject Him because of the things we don't understand.

Rabbi Yani deserves a place in our study—but only at the end, after we've opened our eyes to the many ways in which we've come to realize that there may be answers or at least partial answers to the problems that so greatly perplex us. Yes, questions remain. For them, we will rely on faith for the answers. But our faith, indeed the faith that Rabbi Yani asks us to grasp, is the faith of a child who understands just a little of where he is going but knows beyond doubt that his Father loves him even when He lets go of his hand for a moment.

It is with this mind-set that we must now approach the most difficult of all the puzzles of evil in history. How can we maintain our faith after the Holocaust?

CHAPTER 15

FAITH AFTER THE HOLOCAUST

How do you make sense of the Holocaust, Rabbi?"

It is a question I dread, but a question I cannot avoid. And it isn't only audiences listening to my lectures who ask it. I doubt if a day has gone by that I haven't asked it of myself as well.

I lost much of my family during that terrible time when God seemed to be absent. My parents thankfully fled to the safety of America, together with my brother, my sister and me. But 6 million weren't so lucky. They were old and young, men and women, little infants. I personally know the meaning of "survivor's guilt." Why me—and not them? Why was I among the fortunate survivors, and why did they perish? I can't believe I am more worthy than them. I have read their stories. I know that among the victims were the pious, the holy, the saintly and the scholars. I wept when I read of their fate. And I wonder, *Why didn't God weep as well? And if He did, how could He have refrained from halting the carnage and from avenging the blood of His children?*

There are some who believe that the Holocaust is no greater a religious challenge than any of the personal issues of suffering endured by anyone. Eliezer Berkovits,[66] for example, argues that, from a theological perspective, the genocide of 6 million people is no different than one child who suffers needlessly or one person who goes through the anguish of personal loss. The theological problem, he says, is the same—injustice. Quantity should make no difference. The issue is: How can a good and just God permit something to happen on Earth that is unjust? The dilemma of Job and the dilemma of the Holocaust are one.

Many others, however, disagree. And I am one of them. The Holocaust as a crime stands *sui generis*—in a category all by itself. Its cruelty, its scope, its numbers and its goal of total annihilation of the Jewish people—all are unparalleled. God's silence as Hitler and his henchmen plotted the "Final Solution" is unique as a divine behavior beyond comprehension.

The extent of the evil that was perpetrated, its impact on the victims as well as the world at large, cannot be underestimated.

Anne Frank touched the hearts of the world. But she was only one. Multiply that 6 million times, and the mind staggers. We cannot possibly comprehend. Add to the number 6 million those whom we call "survivors," but who could never survive their daily nightmares and their ongoing memories of hell. They didn't "survive" as much as they went on living, forever scarred by evil that goes far beyond human imagination.

That's why I maintain that to treat genocide on a par with the pain of a single individual is to minimize and cheapen the Holocaust. The two cannot be compared. To do so is simply offensive.

I am pained whenever I see that Holocaust terminology has crept into everyday language. All too frequently we read about oppressed people enduring various degrees of difficulty, and the word "Holocaust" is bandied about as if the term implied no more than economic deprivation or physical hardship. It's gotten so that we have environmentalists describing the disappearing rainforests as an Ecological Holocaust and the "Save the Whales" groups warning of the pending extinction of these aquatic animals as an Oceanic Holocaust.

Without a doubt, other groups of people have suffered terribly and in no way do I want to minimize their pain. Croats have been victims of ethnic cleansing campaigns by the Serbs. Armenians suffered a genocidal massacre under the Turks. Pol Pot largely succeeded in exterminating the intelligentsia of Cambodia. But none of those events can come close to the evil perpetrated during the Holocaust.

These days we even read about the Palestinian Holocaust, an idea popularized by Palestinian groups to try and accuse the state of Israel of treating them in the same way that the Nazis treated the Jews. Even when the worst crimes by Jews against Palestinians are considered—such as the massacre of twenty-nine Moslems by Baruch Goldstein in the Cave of the Patriarchs—there is nothing that comes anywhere near the crimes of Nazi Germany. Theirs was a *national* (and later international) policy by a government to exterminate an entire people from the face of the Earth. It was a policy that included the torture, starvation and, finally, the massacre of children as well as adults.

I don't want to belabor the point, but I think the prevailing view among the world's historians is that in the wide range of experiences of evil throughout all of history, the Holocaust stands separate, apart, distinct and alone. There is nothing like it in terms of other genocides or massacres of the past, not even in comparison with Jewish suffering such as the Inquisition of Spain or the pogroms of Russia. The Holocaust was the unique contribution of "civilized" twentieth-century man.

It is with regard to the Holocaust that our question becomes all the more urgent, the more puzzling and the more relevant: Where was God?

THE QUESTIONS WITHIN THE QUESTION

Theologians have pointed out that there are really three questions within this question. We must consider where God was before, during and after the Holocaust. To break it down:

1. What was God's role before the event? That is to say, did He take part in the decision to let it occur?

2. Where was God during the Holocaust? In other words, was He there in the midst of the horrors and the terrible suffering? And if so, what was His reaction? If fathers and mothers who witnessed the brutal murder of their child went insane, then our question is, "God, You are our father. You are our mother. How could You watch it and not do something?"

3. And finally, what was God's role after the Holocaust? In the aftermath of evil on this grand scale, can Jews go on keeping God's commandments as if nothing had happened to shake their faith?

By now, more than half a century after the event, many have struggled with these questions. Some religious thinkers, like Reform Rabbi Richard Rubenstein, decided that after Auschwitz they could no longer retain their faith. Together with a number of survivors, their belief was irrevocably shattered.

Yet I also know people who endured these horrors, witnessed the worst of man's evil firsthand and came out with a stronger faith in God than before.

Elie Wiesel, the Nobel Prize–winning chronicler of the Holocaust who went through his own very public period of questioning, remains a deeply religious man. While still troubled by the inexplicable silence of God, Wiesel refuses to renounce his connection with the Almighty. He chooses instead to identify with the survivors whose story he immortalized.

It is a scene Wiesel captured at the conclusion of a very famous lecture on the Holocaust. His account movingly describes the conflicting feelings of those who almost miraculously survived. Wiesel speaks about what the Jews had endured. Then he recounts what happened on the day his concentration camp was liberated. The American Army came in and freed the survivors. At that moment, everyone responded to freedom in a different way. Some rushed out to find Germans to kill, to take revenge. Others hurried out to find food, to sate the hunger that had for so long defined their existence. Still others rushed to plunder and steal. They felt something was owed them; they had been robbed of everything, literally of life, and they went out to grab what they could to make up for what was taken from them.

Wiesel depicts the people running in different directions. Then he adds,

> *But there remained one group, a large group, who gathered together and without telling each other what they were going to do—it was so automatic—these people began to pray, to recite* kaddish, *the mourning prayer, which is, in fact, a song of praise to God.*
>
> *This was the mourning prayer for those who weren't going to walk out of there—for husbands, mothers, fathers, for children, for the ones that they had seen killed, for German Jewry, Hungarian Jewry, Polish Jewry, a prayer for 6 million dead.*
>
> *Clearly, after all the horrors, these people still found the strength to pray for those they lost and to praise God.*

Then Wiesel paused for a long time. There was dead silence in the room.

Finally, he said, "In my opinion, God did not deserve that *kaddish*." And he walked off the stage.

It was a serious and public indictment. And yet, Wiesel still studies the Talmud, still puts on *teffilin*. He has not lost his faith. And that is probably the most remarkable part of the story—for Wiesel, and for the Jewish people as well. No matter how severely we might view God's behavior, we aren't willing to sever our relationship.

"WE CAN ONLY ASK"

How did Wiesel resolve his argument with God? How did he find the ability to continue to worship a God who seemed to have forsaken him? What was *his* answer to the problem of God's silence in the face of such incredible suffering?

Wiesel offers a remarkable response.

After the Holocaust, he writes, every one of us has 6 million questions we are entitled to ask God. But we do not ask them in order to be given justifications for God's actions. We do not question in order to hear explanations. Quite the contrary, Wiesel claims, arguments justifying God in the face of evil are not only inadequate, they are diabolical. Answers, he asserts, cannot come from man but only from God Himself. What then is the role for us? Not to explain, but only to ask!

In his bestselling work *Night,* Wiesel recalls that this is the lesson that Moshe the Beadle taught him when he was a young boy in Sighet: "Man raises himself toward God by the questions he asks Him. That is the true dialogue. Man questions God, and God answers. But we don't understand His answers. We can't understand them because they come from the depths of the soul, and they stay there until death."

It is in this vein that Wiesel included the following prayer in *The Six Days of Destruction:* "We do not demand answers, God. But if this is the last page of the human chronicles, assure us that we had the right to ask."

Indeed, there are those, like Wiesel, who find sufficient comfort in merely verbalizing their bewilderment. Answers are more than irrelevant; they are impossible. Faith will have to bear the entire weight of confusion.

For them there is no point in proceeding. We match God's silence with our own. And in silence we bear our pain—and continue to pray.

But for many others, this simply isn't sufficient. After all, we have developed a number of models to explain suffering in former times. Can't any of them be applied to this historic event as well? Are all the insights of the past inapplicable to the Holocaust? In the more than fifty years since we've been trying to reconcile faith with the facts of the "Final Solution," we've heard a number of different possible explanations. Let's follow their arguments carefully and see if we can agree with any of them—or perhaps come to some conclusions of our own.

But before we do, we need to introduce a word of caution.

TALMUDIC WORDS OF CAUTION

Of course, the Talmud was written many centuries before the Holocaust. But the Talmud[67] may present us with a model for how we should approach the Holocaust question in its discussion of the attempted genocide of the Jewish people at the time of the Persian Empire. At that time, as recounted in the book of Esther, the evil Haman convinced King Ahasuerus to issue an edict condemning all Jews to death.

Studying this tale four hundred years after the event, the students of Rabbi Shimon Ben Yochai asked, "Why were the 'Jewish enemies' deserving of destruction in that generation of Esther?" Note that even though hundreds of years had passed, the subject is still so sensitive that they dare not ask, "Why were the *Jewish people* deserving of destruction in the generation of Esther?" even though that was what they meant.

Instead, they ask the question obliquely, by way of a euphemism: "Why were the Jewish enemies . . . ?" But, of course, what they really wanted to know was, "Why did the Jews almost die in the days of Haman? What could they possibly have done to deserve this fate?"

The Talmud records the discussion that followed.

First, their teacher Rabbi Shimon Ben Yochai says to them, "Let me hear what you have to say."

Now the students begin to speculate. Perhaps it was because they (the Jews) had partaken in the feast of an evil man. The book of Esther begins with the description of a luxurious feast prepared by the king for the people of his capital city of Shushan. All were invited, and Jews participated. Perhaps that was their crime: They ate nonkosher food and enjoyed it, no less. Perhaps they had too good a time in exile, partying when they should have been mourning the loss of their land.

But the rabbi doesn't buy any of it. He says, "If indeed they committed that crime, then they should have died." But, he emphasizes, the outcome was quite different. They didn't die. Furthermore, to disprove this theory, the death decree was issued against all Jews, not just the sinners who committed what you use as justification for the potential genocide.

Letting the students mull that one over, he then offers this explanation: "The death decree was the result of idol worship." And he goes on: "The Jews bowed to idols, but they only acted outwardly. When they bowed to an idol, they didn't really believe in their hearts that they were bowing to a god. They bowed from without but not from within. The sin was merely on the surface. So the Holy One, Blessed be He, only allowed a threat to their survival that on the surface seemed perilous but in reality was never consummated."

His explanation goes along with a principle we considered early on in this book—measure for measure. Their act of idolatry was in appearance only. Therefore, too, the decree of death was in appearance only. It was issued, but not carried out.

What I find so very noteworthy in this discussion is the remarkable restraint of the rabbis in their approach to the topic. Rabbi Shimon Ben Yochai, who had what he considered

a possible solution, wanted first to teach his students how difficult it is to find the right answers and how hesitant one must
be in suggesting a theologically satisfying response. And let
it be remembered that this was more than four hundred years
after the event!

I cannot stress this enough—four hundred years after the
near extermination of the Jewish people, Talmudic greats had
a hard time facing the issue head-on. They approached it
obliquely and had to struggle for answers. But we are trying
to make sense of a genocide that *did* happen, and we are trying to do so not even one hundred years after the event. The
challenge is more than formidable.

But we dare not avoid it. As I've already made clear, for
theologians, or for that matter anyone struggling to maintain
faith in a caring God, the Holocaust represents the ultimate
challenge. As Frederick Buechner put it:

> *It is impossible to think about the Holocaust. It is impos-
> sible not to think about it. Anyone who claims to believe in an
> all-powerful, all-loving God without taking into account this
> devastating evidence either that God is indifferent or power-
> less, or that there is no God at all, is playing games. If love is
> really at the heart of it all, how can such things happen? What
> do such things mean?*

So let us face up to the challenge.

There are a number of very interesting approaches that have
been taken in trying to answer the large question: "Where was

God before, during and after the Holocaust?" We can categorize these attempts to make sense of the Holocaust according to five archetypal models drawn from the treasure house of Jewish thought and wisdom. I'd like to analyze with you what I think we can agree with and what I believe we must reject in these five ways of coming to terms with God's actions.

HOLOCAUST AS PUNISHMENT

Our first model—Model A—is Adam. This model I call the "formula of sin and punishment." Adam, who sinned by violating God's command, is expelled from the Garden of Eden and is punished. This is a classic pattern that appears frequently in the Torah. Man does something wrong and suffers the consequences.

For some, this seems to be the most obvious way of understanding the Holocaust. Like Adam, the victims of genocide must have done something wrong. What makes this approach so improbable—and, better put, objectionable—is its willingness to accept the possibility that *any* sin could have been sufficiently evil to warrant God countenancing the Holocaust.

Could there have been a sin committed that was enormous enough to justify a punishment that caused the death of 6 million Jews, gathered together from different countries, to be murdered only because they shared one characteristic—that they were Jews? Even if there were a sin heinous enough, is it conceivable that all Jews were equally culpable? And indeed even if we were to identify such a sin among *all Jews* of that time, what about the tiny infants and small children? Why were the innocent punished—if indeed they were punished—along with the guilty?

For those still willing to adopt the model of Holocaust as punishment, the only response to these last seemingly irrefutable objections is that when enough people in the community sin, God's wrath is unleashed. And then the wicked are punished along with the guilty—all are caught up in a web of destruction. I frankly cannot subscribe to such a view. I can't believe that Abraham was wrong when he rhetorically asked God, in his pleas for the people of Sodom and Gomorrah, "If there are fifty righteous people in the city, will you wipe away the righteous with the wicked? Shall the judge of the whole world not act in accord with justice?"

Putting aside that stricture, though, the first and most direct question remains: What sin could possibly have been immense enough to convince God to turn His back on His people?

Remarkably enough, two prominent rabbinic figures of the past generation dared to suggest an answer. Each one identified a different sin. And, strangest of all, their opinions are the mirror opposites of each other.

Rabbi Joel Teitlelbaum of Satmar, known as the Satmar Rebbe, was the chief spokesman for the view that Zionism is the great collective sin of the Jews in the twentieth century. In his words, "The attempt to hasten the final redemption by immigrating to the land of Israel en masse before the coming of Messiah is the sin that brought this tragedy about."[68]

What, you ask, could possibly have led a rabbi to such a strange conclusion? His argument, he claimed, is based on the Talmudic maxim[69] that the Jewish people swore two oaths before God as they entered the second exile:

1. That Israel would not "go up like a wall" [conquer Israel by massive force]
2. That they would not rebel against the nations of the world [would obey the governments in the exile]

Zionism, the Satmar Rebbe declares, is the Jewish negation of these sacred oaths. It deserves the most severe punishment because it violates a national commitment to wait for divine redemption.

But what the Satmar, as well as his disciples (known as the *Neturey Karta*), ignore is the conclusion of that very same passage. There was in fact *a third oath,* an oath that God imposed upon the non-Jewish world amongst whom the Jews would live in their exile. God made the non-Jews swear not to oppress Israel or try to exterminate them. And the oaths were interdependent; they are binding only if there is mutual observance of its demands by both parties to the contractual agreement.

Even if the Talmudic passage is meant to be taken literally— an interpretation that many scholars dispute—its demand for Jews not to "go up like a wall" was rendered moot by the oppression Jews faced from the nations into which they were exiled.

More serious still—by way of objection to this approach—
is the contention that the desire of the Jewish people to return
to their ancient homeland could possibly constitute a sin of
major proportion. The majority of Jewish thinkers, basing
themselves on a host of traditional sources, disagree with the
position that Jews were meant to sit and wait for God to
deliver us without our involvement. Quite the contrary. God
made us partners in the work of redemption. The Messiah is
God's gift to a world that proves it actively works for his
speedy arrival.

To blame the Holocaust on the Zionists seems more than
outlandish; for many, myself included, it is even blasphemous.

Perhaps it isn't surprising then that within the very same
model of "Holocaust as punishment" we find an explanation
that is diametrically opposed to the Satmar Rebbe. There are
some who have expressed the belief that the victims of the
Holocaust were indeed punished by God—not because they
were Zionists, but precisely because they failed to support
Zionism.

This approach is most vividly articulated in the book
Happy Is the Mother of Sons by Rabbi Yissochor Solomon
Pechtal, a book that enjoyed a very large readership after the
Holocaust.

Rabbi Pechtal writes that those who failed to subscribe to
the idea of Zionism and refused to settle in what was then
Palestine perished. The ones who willingly chose to preserve
the Diaspora instead of taking advantage of the opportunity to

dwell in the Promised Land proved to be victims of the Nazis' viciousness.

As he explains it, God remembered the people of Israel, and a call went out for them to leave their exile and emigrate to the land of Israel. This happened in the early 1900s when the British Empire conquered the Ottoman Empire, and Palestine was available for occupancy by Jewish people. Many Jews did go back to their homeland, then, but not enough. Those who did survived the Holocaust. Those who did not died. The crime is seen as not heeding God's call; the punishment, extermination at the hands of the Nazis.

Now in contrast to the Satmar Rebbe's argument that was disseminated some years after the Holocaust, Rabbi Pechtal's was written and printed in Hungary while the Holocaust raged. The author wrote with full knowledge of what was happening. His argument is supported by numerous citations from Midrashic sources, as well as by historic analysis of the opportunities for returning to the land of Israel, which were fatally missed.

So we have completely different conclusions from two learned scholars, both of whom see the Holocaust in terms of sin and punishment. It is fascinating to note that both of them were Hungarian, raised in the same culture, learned in the same texts and schooled in similar Yeshivot. Yet, as we've seen, their opinions differed so radically.

And this is why neither one of these explanations—indeed the entire model of sin and punishment—convinces me. If

God wanted to punish people for a sin committed—if He wanted to proclaim, "I will show you! You will never do that again!"—would His message have been so muddled? If God's purpose was to prove to us the error of our ways, is it possible for it to have been communicated in a manner that leaves us so confused as to its meaning?

I have to believe that His message as punishment would have followed the standard God utilized throughout the Bible. It would have come across loud and clear. It wouldn't have allowed for diametrically opposite interpretations. Punishment without a clear purpose renders it meaningless.

Add to all this perhaps the most telling point: Is it conceivable that, whatever God's view of Zionism, pro or con, an error of judgment on the part of the Jews makes them legitimate victims of German brutality and genocide?

Interestingly, there is yet a third explanation that uses the idea of sin and punishment as its model. Scholars who subscribe to this line of thinking see the sin as having nothing to do with Zionism but rather with the rampant rise of assimilation. They point to the fact that Germany, post-Enlightenment, was a magnet for Jews to leave their religious tradition and to begin a process of alienation from, and denial of, Judaism. So, the proponents of this view say, God reacted according to the principle of measure for measure. As Jews abandoned God, He abandoned them. In the very place where Jews swore to be "more German than the Germans" and proclaimed themselves to be "not Jews, but

Germans of the Mosaic persuasion," God remained silent when the Germans turned on the Jews.

While this argument follows the same sin/punishment model, it is formulated differently from the others. According to this approach, the Holocaust as the plan for an end to Jewish survival merely fulfilled the very same goal as the German Jews aspired to themselves. If the Holocaust had not brought about the physical annihilation of the Jews, they would, in any case, have suffered spiritual annihilation. Jews would have in any event died out by way of assimilation, which is to say, by their own hand. God "beat them to the punch," so to speak, making sure they died as Jews rather than living on as assimilated non-Jews.

Oddly, this argument is advanced not only by religious scholars, but secular ones as well. Most prominent among them was Isaac Tabenkin, a staunch socialist. Speaking at the 26th Zionist Congress, he said: "I feared a Holocaust. I knew there would be one. I feared assimilation even more. Is there anything worse than the destruction of the Jews? Assimilation is part of the destruction of the Jews. A Jew who has been killed has not assimilated."

Where this argument fails is that countless numbers of those who perished had not tried to assimilate. They were as religious, and as Jewish, as ever. Of course, the proponents of this view answer that once a fire rages, it rages out of control. The Holocaust began in Germany as God's way of dealing with assimilation. Subsequently, it got out of hand.

I cannot buy this argument. That would suggest that God is not all-powerful. It suggests that things can get out of God's control. It fails the crucial test we outlined at the beginning of this book. It doesn't allow for the acceptance of the crucial ideas that define our faith: that God is just and that God is omnipotent.

Richard Rubinstein, in his daring work, *After Auschwitz: Radical Theology and Contemporary Judaism,* pioneered the heretical idea that "God is dead" after the Holocaust precisely because he took for granted the sin/punishment model:

> *I believe the single greatest challenge to modern Judaism arises out of the question of God and the death camps. How can Jews believe in an omnipotent, beneficent God after Auschwitz? Traditional Jewish theology maintains that God is the ultimate, omnipotent actor in the historical drama. It has interpreted every major catastrophe in Jewish history as God's punishment of a sinful Israel. I fail to see how this position can be maintained without regarding Hitler and the S.S. as instruments of God's will. The idea is simply too obscene for me to accept.*

This is also why I cannot subscribe to the sin/punishment model. At its core, it is a model that transfers guilt from the perpetrators to the people who perished. It turns the villains into agents of God. It justifies the unjustifiable. I agree that this approach is obscene. Where Rubenstein errs, though, is in assuming that this model is the *only* way Jewish theology explains catastrophes. There are in fact other alternatives.

HOLOCAUST AS AN EXPRESSION OF FREE WILL

The second model—Model B—has its source in the story of Cain and Abel.

Cain, the first murderer in history, carried out an act contrary to the will of God. Indeed, God was angered by what occurred. Yet, as we clearly see from the story, God allowed it to happen. Cain exercised his free will. Therefore, God has no culpability in the death of Abel. It was Cain who killed Abel, not God.

Of course, God didn't want Abel dead. But had God intervened to save Abel, He would have had to deprive Cain of his free will. That, we've already explained, wasn't an option because God values man's free will more than His own desires. That makes it possible for Cain to succeed and evil to become reality.

According to this model, the Nazis were Cain.

In this view, the Holocaust is not a question that should be addressed to God. It's an accusation that should be directed to man.

Abraham Joshua Heschel made the point starkly:[70]

> *Our world seems not unlike the pit of snakes. We did not sink into the pit in '39 or even in '33. We had descended into it*

generations ago. The snakes have sent their venom into the bloodstreams of humanity, gradually paralyzing us, numbing nerve after nerve, dulling our minds, darkening our vision. The outbreak of war was no surprise. It came as a long expected sequel to a spiritual disaster. Man went wrong. Man went bad. Man went very, very bad. Man went totally bad. Men committed the Holocaust.

Blaming God is to adopt the very same tack as Cain did when his crime was discovered. Cain asked, "Am I my brother's keeper?" The words seem ludicrous at first glance. Cain had just killed. Surely he realized that God was aware of that as well. How dare he ask if he is obligated to be his brother's keeper? Even if he were exempt from that task, he's not allowed to murder his brother!

There is a Midrash[71] that helps us make sense of these words of Cain.

Here is what Cain really meant when he said, "Am I my brother's keeper?"

"God, You are the guardian of all creatures. You are omnipotent. You can certainly do whatever you want. Had you really wanted my brother not to die, it was in your hands to stop me. Am *I* my brother's keeper? No, *You are.* Don't blame me. If you let it happen, you must have agreed. You're just as guilty as I am—if not more so."

Then the Midrash goes on to compare the relationship between Cain and God to a thief and a watchman. It presents this parable. A thief stole some vessels in the night. In the morning the watchman confronts him: "Why did you steal the vessels?" And the thief replies: "I am a thief. I did my business. I only exercised my skill. You are a watchman. Your duty is to keep guard at the gates. Why did you not use your skill?"

So this is what Cain was saying to God. "You created me as I am—a human being with an evil inclination. I acted accordingly. And You, the guardian of all creatures, allowed me to kill. I am not my brother's guardian, You are."

The Biblical text doesn't even bother to respond to this indictment of God. Cain's words can only come from a criminal looking to excuse his actions in the classic way—shifting the blame. It may even sound like there's some logic to it, but Cain's case is based on a totally false assumption. God's failure to stop evil isn't the same as acquiescence. Cain's accusation of God was the ultimate *chutzpah:* turning God's gift of free will into an argument for God's agreement to murder.

What Cain forgot is the premise of free will. To allow man to choose forces a measure of passivity on God. But that doesn't mean evil won't eventually be held accountable. Sin is possible, not permissible. And God? What will He do? God will pronounce judgment. God will decree that Cain become a wanderer over the face of the Earth. And on Cain's forehead, God will place a sign branding him as a murderer. It may not happen immediately, but justice will eventually triumph.

The Holocaust, according to this approach, was the temporary victory of evil not because of God's wickedness, but because of His grace—His goodness in giving human beings the gift that allows them to become angels or devils.

Perhaps even more, the Holocaust *affirmed* a fundamental truth that makes Judaism all the more relevant. It proved the failure of *man without the spiritual teachings of God.* What the world witnessed in the 1940s was how low it could sink when it forsakes ethics and law as well as the moral conscience that has been the greatest gift of the Jews to mankind. Far from de-legitimatizing God, the Holocaust made clear that without Him and His teachings, the Earth could not survive.

This is an approach that I find fairly compelling. If the first model of sin/punishment proved unacceptable, the free will theory has much to commend it. It's hard to accept this as a complete explanation for the Holocaust, though, given the extent of its horrors. Does free will really demand God's total abdication? How then do we explain divine intervention throughout the course of history? Didn't those moments prove that there *are* crimes sufficiently worthy of His intercession? Is it possible that God took a perpetual vow of passivity? And if there were times when God was angry enough, upset enough, livid enough to override the results of free will, didn't the horrors of the Holocaust warrant the same kind of response?

Perhaps yet a third model for God's ways can help us deal with our difficulty.

HOLOCAUST AS TEST

The third model—Model C—is based on the story of Abraham. The Bible teaches that Abraham had to face ten trials, the last of which was that he was asked to sacrifice his son Isaac. It seems incomprehensible that God should ask a man to offer up his own child as proof of his faith. But then again, aren't tests—by their very nature—always incomprehensible? If Abraham would have known it was a test, the Divine request would not have represented a challenge of devotion.

Perhaps, some say, the story of Abraham's sacrifice of Isaac represents a preview of the twentieth-century event that similarly required a supreme test of our faith in the face of the incomprehensibility of the Holocaust. Terrible and frightening, yes, but the more difficult the test, the greater the reward. Abraham's story demonstrates that trials can well be part of the religious experience. Isn't it possible that the Holocaust was the collective *Akeidah* story, forcing us as a people to prove ourselves in the very same way as our patriarch?

The idea at first glance seems to possess some merit. But there is an obvious difference between the two events. In Abraham's story, at the critical moment when Abraham lifted his sword to complete the test, the Torah tells us that God sent an angel to say, "Stop!"

In the Holocaust, there was no angel. There was no order from God to halt. Instead, the lifted sword did descend, and the blood of 6 million flowed to the Earth.

The differences between the reality and the model outweigh any apparent similarities. It simply doesn't make sense. It doesn't apply from the perspective of Abraham because then the Nazis would have to be compared to this saintly man who obeyed the voice of God. And it doesn't apply from the perspective of Isaac, who, although he was willing to give up his life, did not die in the end.

Tests are supposed to serve a purpose. Tests are meant to be constructive, not destructive. That makes it almost impossible to believe that the Holocaust can be explained by the model of the test of Abraham.

Thus we move on to the next model.

HOLOCAUST AS MESSIANIC PREREQUISITE

This model—Model D—bases itself on the Messianic visions of the prophets.

It is from the Biblical writings of many of the spokesmen for God who talk of "the end of days" that we hear of a concept known as *chevley leydah,* "the birth pangs of the Messiah." The prophets Zechariah, Malachi, Joel and others predicted that the time immediately preceding the final redemption would be filled with death and destruction on a scale almost unimaginable. So frightening is their description that the Talmud[72] tells of scholars who declared that they hoped Messiah would come, but that they themselves would not live to witness his arrival. "Of course, we would love to be a part of the Messianic age," they explained, "but we cannot endure the thought of having to witness the days that will immediately precede his coming."

In the sixteenth century, Rabbi Judah Loew, better known as "The Maharal of Prague," wrote at length concerning the kinds of events that will herald the coming of the Messiah on the basis of these predictions. The Maharal warned of a period of crisis—a crisis on many levels. Yet, he concluded, salvation will arise precisely as a result of this crisis. In the words of the Maharal, "From amidst nothingness, life will be born."

His words foreshadow both the Holocaust as well as the birth of Israel that followed shortly thereafter. His elaboration of Biblical predictions is harrowing in its depiction of the horrors that were so accurately fulfilled during the Holocaust. What makes his words all the more remarkable is the realization that, as the prophets indeed indicated, the tragedy in fact proved to be the harbinger of the miraculous return of the Jewish people to their land after almost two thousand years of exile.

The comparison to a woman giving birth—the screams of pain followed by overwhelming joy—proved to be an appropriate metaphor. Given the choice, we too might have agreed with the rabbis of the Talmud who prayed that they not be alive in the generation preceding redemption. Yet, as Elie Wiesel so beautifully put it, "We are the most cursed of all generations, and we are the most blessed of all generations. We are the generation of Job, but we are also the generation of Jerusalem."

How are we to explain this strange linkage? What is it that creates the connection between unparalleled pain and unbounded joy? Why did the prophets see the imminence of a holocaust prior to a return to our national homeland?

The answer is far from clear.

Some, like the famous scholar Rabbi Yonathan Eibeshutz, have tried to understand it by way of analogy:

Just as the night precedes the day, and the present world precedes the world-to-come, so, too, it is only fitting that the redemption be preceded by darkness. Every new existence spells the end of preceding existence. This is the reason for the void before the appearance of the Messiah, to the point where all previous existence dissolves. Only then does existence begin anew. This is the reason that the sages teach in the Talmud:[73]

> *Rabbi Yochanan said that in the generation in which the son of David [i.e., the Messiah] comes, the number of Torah scholars will decrease, and the eyes of those who remain will become weak from grief and groaning, and great hardships and severe decrees will be renewed; no sooner does one pass than a new one arises. [It is further written there,] Rabbi Yehuda says that in the generation in which the son of David comes, the meeting place [of Torah scholars] will be [used] for prostitution, the*

> *Galilee will be destroyed, the Gavlan will be deserted, and the people of the Galilee will wander from city to city and will not be comforted, the wisdom of the sages will decrease, the sin-fearing will be despised, the face of the generation will resemble the face of a dog, and truth will be hard to come by. . . .*

The terrible hardships we experienced in Europe during the Second World War may have served as part of the fulfillment of this very dire forecast. The Holocaust represented an aspect of the "void" prior to the "rebirth" of the Jewish people in the land of Israel. The "coincidence" of the calendar that placed the Holocaust in such close proximity to the creation of the State of Israel is surely something that demands our attention. It must carry with it a divine message.

Can that serve as a source of comfort? Is it enough to give us a measure of consolation for our grievous losses? While for many the idea of "the birth pangs of Messiah" fails to offer an acceptable rationale, we should note that during the Holocaust itself there were rabbis who calmed their disciples as they marched to their deaths by telling them to think of their suffering as the sacrifices that would hasten the arrival of the Redeemer.

The most unbearable of all deaths is the death that is viewed as meaningless. To believe that dying serves a purpose is to invest it not only with meaning but also with holiness. That is what this model was able to achieve for some victims. They may not have understood the "why" of their sacrifice, but they did believe in its significance. And that allowed them to go to their deaths with dignity.

Is this approach enough for us as we grapple with the theological difficulties of the Holocaust? If it doesn't satisfy us as an answer, it permits us at the very least to recognize that the incomprehensible was nevertheless part of a divine plan already revealed thousands of years ago to the prophets. It transforms tragedy into a stepping-stone for ultimate blessing. And that surely brings with it a measure of consolation.

HOLOCAUST AS UNEXPLAINABLE

And, finally, we come back full circle to the model of Job—Model E.

In this model we acknowledge the apparent lack of justice in God's behavior. But as the book of Job teaches us, no matter what effort man makes to comprehend God's ways, he will not succeed. Job never does get an answer to his questions. God's answer—as we noted in chapters 1 and 14—is only a string of questions that underscores how woefully limited human beings are in contrast to the awesome power of God:

Where were you when I laid the Earth's foundations? . . . Can you send up an order to the clouds for an abundance of water to cover you? . . . Can you hunt prey for the lion and satisfy the appetite of the king of beasts? . . . Is it by your wisdom that the hawk grows pinions, spreads his wings to the south?[74]

In other words, God says to Job, I run this vast and complicated world, and you cannot possibly grasp the multitude of reasons why I do what I do.

And so Job, hearing all that, concludes: "Behold, I am of small account. What shall I answer You? I lay my hand upon my mouth."

Oddly, Job has been comforted by this non-answer to his question, and he agrees to question no further. That is Job's attitude at the end, after all his harrowing experiences.

Now you can say that this is a cop-out. How can there be any comfort in this non-answer? Or you can look at this from a higher perspective and accept it as answer by way of submission to a superior intelligence that runs the world in a manner we cannot fathom.

For example, if someone were to say, "Obviously, my doctor is wrong because I do not understand his prescription," you would respond, "That's absurd! Your statement doesn't make sense because here you are going to a specialist with a knowledge you don't possess."

As Maimonides says, at times the doctor's medicine may be amputation of a limb, something that seems very cruel to a primitive person who has no knowledge of the workings of modern medicine. Yet the doctor could not explain to the patient why and how gangrene spreads. They would lack a common language. The best the doctor could say would be, "As strange as it seems, this is good for you."

In the same way, terrible things that happen are in some

strange way that we do not understand in our best interest. And only a superior intelligence knows why. As the Bible says, "The secret things belong to the Lord, our God."[75]

The relevance of this idea to the Holocaust was made clear to me some years ago in one of the most incredible experiences of my life. I want to share it with you in the next chapter with the hope that it fortifies your faith in the face of the inexplicable as it did mine.

CHAPTER 16

A MEETING WITH
A MYSTIC

A chance meeting with a mystic changed my life.

Some years ago, I was in Israel on a congregational tour when a friend shared with me some remarkable stories about a saintly scholar in the city of Safed. Those who knew him well were sure that he was one of those known in Jewish tradition as "the thirty-six righteous men"—those thirty-six holy people in whose merit the entire world is maintained.

I could not dare hope that I would have the opportunity to actually meet him, but fate and divine destiny somehow brought us together. The details of our meeting were so incredible that I have to believe God Himself brought it about. But what I learned after we spent memorable hours together has indelibly altered the way I now understand the Bible, religion and, indeed, even life itself.

Why he took me into his confidence, I still do not know. He is a man utterly immune to the enticements of fame and

215

wealth. He shared with me a mystical "secret" on two conditions: that I not reveal it publicly until he informs me that the time is ripe and that I never, ever divulge his identity and disturb his lifelong pursuit of anonymity.

For years, I kept the "secret" to myself. It allowed me to see things as no one else did. Yet I could not say a word because of my promise.

And then one year he called and told me simply, "Now is the time." I have no idea what has changed. Perhaps it is because the world is today more attuned to the mystical and more receptive to its profound teachings. Perhaps it is because people have already been introduced to the concept of Biblical codes and will not be overly cynical about a somewhat comparable approach. Or perhaps it is because there is something this secret can teach us today that the world desperately needs for its enlightenment, for its inspiration and for its very survival.

Let me therefore share it with you precisely the way I heard it.

We had spoken of miracles. He told me that miraculous events did not end with Biblical tales. They are ongoing, throughout all of history, including modern times. The creation of the State of Israel, for example, he said, happened as an expression of God's will exactly when it was predicted to occur in the Bible.

"Predicted exactly when it was supposed to?" I asked. "I don't recall the promise of return to the land being identified with a specific year."

"Then perhaps," he replied, "it is time for me to reveal to you the secret of sentences."

I had no idea what he meant. Sentences? What secret could he possibly be referring to? "Let me show you something," he told me. And then he confided in me an insight he had received from his teachers that literally left me gasping.

"The year the State of Israel was born was 1948 in the secular calendar. In our traditional way of counting, the date was 5708. Know that the verses in the five books of Moses, the Torah, correspond to the years of history. Every major event of all times will have some allusion to it, direct or indirect, in the verse which is linked to it by number. Do you know," he asked me, "what the 5,708th verse in the Bible is?"

Of course, I had no idea.

So he told me, and I subsequently verified it by lengthy counting. "It is Deuteronomy 30:3: 'And the Lord your God will turn your captivity and have compassion upon you, and will return and gather you from all the peoples where the Lord your God has scattered you.'"

It was amazing. And it seemed too good to be true. Perhaps it was just a remarkable coincidence, one of those accidents that are more entertaining than instructive. But it was certainly intriguing: The one verse that speaks of return to the land after centuries of exile is actually the very same number Biblical sentence as the year in which this unlikely event occurred!

So I found the nerve to ask a follow-up question. "You

mean," I haltingly inquired, "this is not simply an isolated instance? It is a principle that relates equally to other major events, and I could for example find a comparable reference to the Holocaust just as well as I did for the time of national redemption?"

"Why not try it yourself?" he responded with a smile. And so I counted the verses backward, making note both of number as well as corresponding year. The previous chapter, chapter 29, was the one whose sentences corresponded to the years of the Holocaust, from the mid-thirties to the end of the Second World War in 5705/1945.

With halting breath, I read the phrases that sprang out at me: "All the curses of the covenant . . . the plagues of that land and the sickness with which the Lord has made it sick . . . the whole land is brimstone and salt and a burning . . . like the overthrow of Sodom and Gomorrah . . . even all the nations shall say, 'Why has the Lord done thus?'"

It was true! The sentences linked by number to the years of the Holocaust described—as if written at the very time the events occurred—the horrors and afflictions of those terrible times.

But there was yet one more amazing revelation that appeared by way of this reading. The verse that corresponds to 5705/1945 stunned me with its powerful message. It is, of course, the sentence that serves as the Torah's final word on the Holocaust and its meaning. It is God's summary as well as His "explanation." And what do the words we are so anxious to hear have to tell us? Listen carefully to the text because I believe it represents the very best and most appropriate judgment that human beings can possibly offer as we consider the events of those days:

> *The secret things belong to the Lord, our God; and the things that are revealed to us and to our children forever are to do all the words of this Law.*[76]

When all is said and done, God is wiser than we are. God understands more than we do. In the profound words of the eleventh-century sage, Bachya Ibn Pakuda, "If we could understand God, we would be God." At times, we may grasp some of His ways. As we probe for reasons and explanations, we can occasionally grab hold of some truths that illuminate God's compassionate guidance of our lives. In those moments, we are overwhelmed by His greatness. And in those times of confusion when we cannot comprehend how God could possibly seem so immune to our suffering, we reassure ourselves that God's love for us is the constant that will never, ever change. The Biblical response to the Holocaust must be our response to the travails of everyday life: "The secret things belong to the Lord, our God."

Our faith is stronger than our misfortunes. Our belief can survive questions that have only partial answers. History may not validate Anne Frank's optimistic judgment that, "In spite of everything, I still believe that people are really good at heart." What I know without doubt, though, is that God is really good at heart, and His "secret things" are the divine methods He uses to bring us back to the paradise He originally created for us.

T his has been a book about questions. Questions that dare to suggest that God's ways may not always be just. Questions that threaten our religious beliefs. Questions that endanger our relationship with the Creator.

We've studied responses from some of the greatest minds of the past. We've learned that not all answers are universally applicable or even satisfying. Some of the insights assuredly resonate more than others. Some ideas will have had meaning to many, others to few or none. As we moved from theme to theme, you will have been the most important judge of the truths that spoke to your heart and helped ease your pain.

After years of counseling people who suffer, I've come to appreciate the wide range of response to the various approaches that have helped people "get through it." What is meaningful to one may seem merely "preachy" to another.

What is profound to one person can seem superficial to somebody else. That's why we've gone through so many different possibilities. My hope in this book—as it is when I speak to people personally—is that you will find at least one thought that strikes with the force of a thunderbolt and that you immediately recognize as *your truth.*

Readers who have gone through the manuscript told me that there was at least one, if not many more, of these flashes of insight that made an idea leap from the page straight into their hearts. As a Hassidic rabbi put it, you will always recognize the truth that applies to your situation by the powerful way that it greets you upon your meeting.

But I don't delude myself into thinking that you will have found in these pages the answers to *all* of your questions. Nor should you despair or be disappointed if you are still troubled by some of God's ways.

Here is a truth that I beg you to remember:

Having questions doesn't make you a nonbeliever. Doubting isn't the same as denying. Religious people are allowed to ask, to be skeptical, yes—even to question God Himself. And that doesn't make them less pious. Quite the opposite. It affirms their faith all the more.

Hard to believe? Let me prove it.

Can faith and doubt co-exist? Does being religious demand the suspension of reason and logic? Is a believer someone who already has all the answers and can never admit to being bewildered by some of God's actions?

Some people might think the answer is obvious. Trust in God, they will tell you, implies unquestioning obedience. Saintliness demands silence. Belief requires blind acceptance.

But they are wrong. And Henry David Thoreau was right when he succinctly said, "Faith keeps many doubts in her pay. If I could not doubt, I should not believe." If you don't think his observation is true, all you have to do is read the Bible. Some of the greatest heroes intuitively understood that if God endowed man with reason, then this divine gift could surely not be sinful. Questioning God isn't a crime; it's just a powerful expression of our awareness that, being created in the image of God, we have an obligation to strive to understand our Creator.

ABRAHAM, THE FIRST MONOTHEIST

Abraham was the first Jew. He was the one to teach the entire world the concept of monotheism. Because of that, God chose to appear to Abraham as friend and confidant. The relationship was so intimate that when God decided he had no choice but to destroy the cities of Sodom and Gomorrah, He made His intentions known to His servant.

"The cries of the cities of Sodom and Gomorrah are exceedingly great, and their sins are truly grievous," God declared. For that reason, they would have to be destroyed. And because Abraham was now so dear to Him, God decided he couldn't hide His plans from His disciple. So Abraham knew what was about to happen.

What took place next is hard to believe. Abraham confronts God. Abraham argues with God. Abraham questions God. "Do you really intend to sweep away the righteous with the wicked? What if there are fifty righteous people in the city? You can't possibly destroy all of them, the good and the bad. That's not like you, God. Far be it from you to do such a thing. Will the judge of the whole world not do justly?"

And how does God respond to this criticism? Amazingly enough, God gives in! All right, He says, if there will be fifty righteous people in the city, I will forgive the entire place for their sake. And Abraham still isn't satisfied. What if there will be only five missing from the total of fifty—will You still destroy all of them simply for the lack of five? To this, too, God accedes. But the discussion isn't over even then. And what if there are only forty? Or thirty? Or twenty, or ten? God accepts this request as well. He will not carry out His plan if even ten righteous people exist. Abraham wins!

How can we possibly understand this story? Is Abraham smarter than the God who created him? Of course not. That certainly isn't the point the text is making. What the Bible is teaching us, according to almost every commentator, is that God took pride in a human being who had the courage to express his convictions. Perhaps this was a test even greater than the one in which Abraham was commanded to bring up his son as an offering. The challenge to Abraham was to define for himself as well as for all of his descendants the proper place for human compassion in the presence of divine judgment. Yes, God decreed, but it was His way of determining how Abraham would respond. Had Abraham passively accepted, placing all his faith in God, God would have lost His faith in Abraham! What the Bible teaches us in this seminal story is that God prefers people of character to pious puppets. Those who have the courage to question are holier than those who believe that God gave us the gift of intelligence but intends for us to never actually use it!

Abraham didn't become a heretic when he voiced his doubts about the justice of God's ways. He knew, of course, that God would have the final say. All he wanted was to be allowed to express his opinion as well. And that isn't just what Abraham wanted. Remarkably enough, that's what God wanted, too.

MOSES ASKED WHY

Moses was the greatest hero in the Bible. He reached a level of prophecy unmatched by anyone before or after. The closing verses of the five books of Moses make clear his uniqueness: "And no prophet arose again in Israel like Moses, whom the Lord knew face to face." If anyone deserves to be called a friend of God, it was surely the man whose face literally shone like a beam of light.

But Moses also understood that even a great friendship with the Almighty didn't preclude him from offering criticism when necessary. After the Jews sinned with the golden calf, God told Moses how angry He was. They are a stiff-necked people, He said, and I am going to consume them. But Moses had the nerve to tell God that he didn't agree. Moses asked questions. They all began with the word why. "Why, O Lord, does your anger wax hot against your people whom you brought forth out of the land of Egypt with great power and with a mighty hand? Why should the Egyptians speak, saying, for evil He brought them out, to slay them in the mountains, and to consume them from the face of the Earth?" In simple language, Moses was almost saying, "God, are you sure you really know what you are doing?"

Daring, isn't it? You would think that this would be counted as a sin for Moses. You might expect God to respond with wrath for such human impertinence. Instead, the Bible concludes this story by telling us that, "The Lord repented of the evil which He said He would do unto His people." Once again, man bests God. The Lord allows a human being to be victorious. And instead of being angry with His servant, we can almost picture God smiling. Moses, just like Abraham before him, realized that questioning God isn't an act of theological *chutzpah*. It is nothing less than an affirmation of human dignity, a valid and praiseworthy demonstration of spiritual courage even in the presence of the Almighty.

Far from being diminished by this seemingly disrespectful outburst, Moses grows in the esteem of the reader as well as of God.

Moses loved God so much, he couldn't bear to remain silent when the Lord's reputation for compassion seemed in jeopardy. Questions, after all, aren't always the same as criticisms. Sometimes they're just another way to ask for clarification. The phrase "Why are you doing this?" needn't be understood as a condemnation. Friends do have a right to react, to be puzzled and to express bewilderment. And that's true, as this story makes clear, even when one of the friends is God Himself.

JOB AND ALL THE OTHER INNOCENTS WHO SUFFER

We know all about Job and his problems. We remember how Job was introduced to us at the beginning of the book named after him not only as someone of exemplary virtue and piety, but also as a person blessed in a manner befitting an individual of his saintliness. We witnessed his fall with sorrow and empathy.

We realize that Job is Everyman. He is the victim who suffers unjustly and cannot believe that God allows his suffering. We recall the friends of Job who tried to convince him that if he was suffering he must've done something to justify it. But Job knew that wasn't true. There is no way that he could accept his horrendous suffering as punishment for crimes he was certain he didn't commit.

For forty-two chapters, the Bible tells us how Job endured. He was a man of wealth who lost all of his possessions. He was the patriarch of a beautiful family now left without descendants. Covered from head to toe with putrid boils that never stopped itching, his feverish body hanging limply on its frame, his eyes sunk back into his head and his ribs protruding from his skin, Job is the paradigm of all those perplexed by their unjust suffering, puzzled by God's seeming lack of compassion and concern for His children.

Job's wife suggested the solution of ultimate despair. "Curse God and die!" In other words, she told her husband: *Why not get it over with? It's no use. There is no future.* Hers was the voice of unmitigated pessimism. Perhaps she was the first advocate of euthanasia. When life offers no alternative to make it worthwhile and faith fails to achieve a positive response, suicide is the only logical answer.

Instead, Job clung to life. He refused to curse God. *But that did not stop him from questioning.* Questioning God isn't the same as denying Him. Quite the contrary. The very act of questioning implies communicating with someone we believe is present and with whom we are certain there is sufficient reason to dialogue. Atheists don't question God because for them there is no one to talk to. Job, on the contrary, knew that no matter how much he suffered, he was not alone. For Job, to question God was to affirm His existence. Of course, Job cried. Of course, he protested, he mourned, he even cursed the day of his birth. But there's one thing he would never do. He would never cross the line and, as his wife suggested, curse God. In the face of all his adversity, he remained firm in his only hope—the very God responsible for his terrible plight.

Job was frustrated, but he didn't lose his faith. Job felt the need to present his case before God because he was confident that he would be vindicated. And when God finally chose to respond, He made clear that from His perspective Job's doubts were more pious than his friends' beliefs. God applauded Job's questions.

That is the message of the book of Job, addressed to everyone who suffers. Pour out your heart to God. Throw out to Him your grief, your anger, your doubt, your bitterness, your betrayal and your disappointment. God is great enough to bear all these and more. The only thing you may not do to God, the one crime for which you will be considered a sinner, *is not to question Him but to ignore Him.*

And that is what the poet Alfred Lord Tennyson understood so well when he wrote, "There lives more faith in honest doubt, believe me, than in half the creeds."

It is this assurance that we can take from the lives of the spiritual giants who preceded us. When we feel deserted by God, we shouldn't consider it blasphemous to repeat the words of King David in his book of Psalms: "My God, my God, why have You forsaken me, far from helping me at the words of my cry? O my God, I call by day but You answer not; and at night, and there is no surcease for me."[77]

"Where are you, God?" is a cry that merges love with frustration, acceptance with bewilderment. It does not diminish our faith. It affirms our relationship even as it attests to our closeness. Only because we love God as much as we do can we feel close enough to ask Him questions!

And that's why I'm sure God won't think any the less of us if we join the company of questioners that includes Abraham and Moses, Job and King David. Who knows? Maybe dealing honestly with our doubts will enable us to strengthen our faith.

That's why we should never be afraid to question. Let's always feel close enough to God to ask. But let's also find strength from those answers that impress us with their truth. And let's live our lives with the confident assurance that the same God who is the source of all of our blessings will also enable us to overcome our sufferings and sorrows.

NOTES

1. Job 1:1.
2. Job 1:21.
3. Job 4:7.
4. Job 38–40.
5. Baba Batra 15a.
6. Genesis 24:1.
7. Baba Metzia 58b.
8. Tractate Berakhot 5a.
9. Genesis 1:1–2.
10. Deuteronomy 32:11.
11. Exodus 21:12–13.
12. As quoted by Rashi.
13. Genesis 17:7 and Leviticus 26:44–45.
14. Esther 4:14.
15. Exodus 33:18–23.
16. Brochot 7a.
17. Pesachim 50a.
18. Chapter 3, law 2.
19. Brochot 60b.
20. Shabbat 55a.
21. Ezekiel 18:20.
22. Psalms 89:33.
23. Numbers 20:12.
24. Other blameless people also died, but by the hand of others; only these four, however, died by the hand of God, although they were totally innocent of sin.
25. Ezekiel 18:20.
26. Numbers 35:9.
27. Ethics of the Fathers 1:12.
28. Jerusalem Talmud, Berakot 2:8.
29. Midrash Rabba 63:12.
30. Genesis 5:24.
31. Ketubot 77b.
32. Midrash Kohelet Raba 7:4.
33. Midrash Mishley 31.

34. Midrash Yalkut Shimeoni, Exodus, Number 398.

35. Winkler, Gershon. *The Soul of the Matter.* Brooklyn, NY: Judaica Press, 1982.

36. Braverman, Rabbi Nachum, *Jewish Journal,* Feb. 14, 1995.

37. Deuteronomy 24:16, Jeremiah 31:29, Ezekiel 18:2, Chronicles II 25:4.

38. Baba Metzia 87a, Sanhedrin 107a.

39. Midrash Rabba 65:9.

40. Genesis 24:1.

41. Genesis 27:1.

42. Genesis 48:1.

43. Taanit 21a, Gittin 14b.

44. Proverbs 3:11–12.

45. Proverbs 13:24.

46. Deuteronomy 8:5.

47. Exodus 15:22–26.

48. Midrash Rabba, Genesis 32:3.

49. Sanhedrin 101a.

50. Rabbi Akiva first quotes a passage from Kings II, Chapter 21, and then expounds upon it.

51. Megillah 14a.

52. Kiddushin 31b.

53. Lamentations 4:11.

54. Sanhedrin 101a.

55. Deuteronomy 7:10.

56. Deuteronomy 4:15.

57. Deuteronomy 11:13–15.

58. Shabbat 127a.

59. Genesis 3:19.

60. Genesis 3:16.

61. Brochot 5a.

62. Isaiah 11:6: "The wolf also shall live with the lamb, and the leopard shall lie down with the kid; and the calf and the young lion and the fatling together; and a little child shall lead them."

63. Nidah 16b.

64. Deuteronomy 34:10–12.

65. Mishna 4:19.

66. Berkovits, Eliezer. *God, Man and History.* Middle Village, NY: Jonathan David Pub., 1979.

67. Megillah 12a.

68. Kuntres Dibros Kodesh 216–217.

69. Ketubot 11a.

70. Heschel, Abraham Joshua, and Susannah Heschel (Ed.). *Moral Grandeur and Spiritual Audacity: Essays.* New York: Noonday Press, 1997.

71. Midrash Hagadol, Bereshit 4:9.

72. Sanhedrin 98b.

73. Sanhedrin 96b, 97a.

74. Job 38–40.

75. Deuteronomy 29:28.

76. Deuteronomy 29:28.

77. Psalms 22:2.

Benjamin Blech is an internationally recognized educator, religious leader, author and lecturer. He is the author of seven highly acclaimed and bestselling books, with combined sales of well over 150,000 copies, including three as part of the highly popular *Idiot's Guide* series. Several of his works have been translated into other languages. *Understanding Judaism: The Basics of Deed and Creed* was chosen by the Union of Orthodox Jewish Congregations as the single best book on Judaism today. Together with an accompanying video, filmed by the producers of *20/20* and featuring Blech, it is presently being used as the basis for study groups in numerous synagogues and universities around the country.

In a national survey (see *www.jewsweek.com*), Blech was ranked #16 in a listing of the fifty most influential Jews in America. A recipient of the American Educator of the Year Award, he has been an associate professor of Talmud at Yeshiva University since 1966.

Blech is Rabbi Emeritus of Young Israel of Oceanside, New York, where he served for thirty-seven years. A tenth-generation rabbi, he has formed thousands of student-teacher relationships through his warm and caring style. Blech is known for his ability to present complicated ideas in a clear and entertaining manner. A past president of both the National Council of Young Israel Rabbis, as well as the International League for the Repatriation of Russian Jewry, Blech has also served as officer for the New York Board of Rabbis as well as the Rabbinical Council of America.

Blech is a frequent lecturer in Jewish communities as far-flung as Australia, South Africa, New Zealand, Bangkok, Singapore, Hong Kong, Tokyo and Israel. Closer to home, he has served as Scholar-in-Residence at hundreds of synagogues throughout the United States and Canada, and has been active on behalf of countless Jewish causes. His lectures on tape have an international following and are among the most popular from among the thousands made available on the Web through *Aish Hatorah (www.aish.com)*.

Blech has appeared on national television (including *Oprah*); hosted a popular weekly radio program in New York; and written for *Newsweek, The New York Times* and *Newsday*, in addition to a wide and varied number of scholarly publications. Blech is an unusually eloquent and gifted speaker, as well as a profound contemporary theologian and religious spokesman who has made a major impact on the many thousands of people he has addressed. His Web site is *www.benjaminblech.com*.